ITALY

FOR
FIRST TIMERS

Everyone deserves an enjoyable, low-stress trip

Italy For First Timers
Lynnette Hartwig
Gettingbestprice.com

Requests for permission should be addressed to the IFFT Permissions Department, 2 Bates Lane, Westford MA 01886 or by email to Lyn8nn@gmail.com.

ISBN: 978-0-9891784-6-4 (paperback) ISBN: 978-0-9891784-5-7 (Digital)
Printed in the United States of America
20 19 18 17 16 15 14 13 12 11 10 9 8 7 6 5

CurrenTech

This book is dedicated to my son, Chapin Johnson.

The light of my life now and for always,

the perfect traveling companion.

Table of Contents

JUST THINKING . . .

Going to Italy! What a happy thought. If you're like me, curiosity about whether the actual trip will match the Italy of the imagination, formed from snips of movies, views from old paintings, scenes from novels and plays is topmost in your mind.

Well, of course it won't. There will be car exhaust and sore feet and Closed for Restoration. But go anyway. Because ten times a day there will be five minutes of . . . that imaginary place. Magical. It doesn't last all day, but in memory it can stretch forever.

This book is about heading off to Italy, but there is plenty more; much applies to all travel in Europe, and much of the information about airlines, hotels and packing applies to all travel. The travel industry has developed protocols and customs which have spread everywhere. They're not intuitive; someone has to tell you the first time or it just doesn't make sense. If you haven't traveled overseas in more than ten years or don't fly much, this book will be a treasure trove.

In this book you get tips on how to get good deals on flight cost and seat availability, the basics of online booking and how to finagle a desirable seat at flight time, even if one wasn't available when you booked.

All the great things your phone can do for you (and one thing it should never do) are in this book, even if you're going to leave it on airplane mode with roaming turned off—plus, how you can have unlimited texting while overseas, even if texting isn't part of your regular package. I don't tell you how to buy an overseas package with your phone company—I leave that to the marketing geniuses at your provider—I tell you how to take a vacation so the phone doesn't cost you a dime extra, yet you keep reasonably in touch, handle local calls, and still get the most out of your amazing Swiss Army Knife of the electronic world.

You'll find the clearest and best pros and cons list for package tours vs. arranging your own. Also in here: the 100% slam dunk no-fail jet lag advice; once I knew this I never had jet lag again, meaning a whole extra useful day in Italy. Try it, you'll like it!

Today, most airlines have weight limits for carry-on items as well as checked bags. While airlines allow 'one luggage and one personal item,' the appearance of the personal item, its shape and how you carry it, makes all the difference in whether you breeze by the airport staff or it causes a hassle. Hassle reduction is the core of this book; when you know what will cause no hassle, some risk of hassle, or huge risk of hassle, you can decide for yourself if it's worth it.

No matter what stage of the trip you're at, from twinkle in your eye to contemplating this in Kindle book format while waiting for dessert in a Venice restaurant, it will improve the quality and enjoyment of your vacation.

The chapter Packing helps you pack only the items you'll use. Packing light and efficiently for today's airline flights, post-2014, is radically different than the oft-repeated, outdated travel advice, dependent upon buying skorts, coordinating colors and wearing scarves, even if you never wear those things in real life.

In addition to hundreds of forever-useful travel tips, there's an easy-to-use list of things to do several weeks before the trip, and then another for things to do a few days before the trip. Forgetting some of these, such as having the post office hold the mail, is not a disaster, but it does take up your mental energy and peace of mind to make arrangements from afar.

On top of those true-for-every-traveler insights, there's plenty that will help you in Italy, such as what you shouldn't bring to Italy (an umbrella) and why there are hundreds of Master locks on the bridge grillwork (you'll see when you get there), and how to get good service in an Italian restaurant. Once you know, you'll wish US restaurants were so considerate.

I'll tell you things that took me so long to search for the answers that I hate handing them to you on a platter. Such as, why are there several prices for seats on a train in Italy, and what's the downside of choosing the cheapest one? Answer: none. They're all the same seats; the difference only shows up when you miss the train, not when you ride it.

When should I buy the city's official Tourist card, and when should I skip it? What's included in the Tourist card? I spend a painful amount of time researching those, visiting multiple review websites and reading hundreds of user comments to flesh out the skimpy website information, yet you will know as much as I do in ten minutes.

This book is the collected wisdom from hundreds of trips. It would take a fast reader dozens of hours online to land upon even 50% of the tips contained here. If your time is worth $5 per hour, this book is worth $200. The real value is more than that; most readers will glean enough key information to save $400 and more from their trip to Italy with no reduction in quality—in fact, quality will increase.

Murano glass is sold all over Venice. You can find whimsical pieces, jewelry, chandeliers, vases and food-serving vessels of all kinds. Last year's pieces are priced to move.

Italy is a great destination for Americans for four reasons. One, you can drink the water with no concerns, the same as anywhere in the US. Two, the food is wonderful to our tastes, thanks to a couple of generations of Italian immigrants who opened restaurants and bakeries. American tastes have been bent more toward Italy than to old England. Which do you eat more often, lamb stew or lasagna? Three, there is so much to see and do. Much of the beautiful and historical artwork is in plazas and public thoroughfares not costing a dime; on the other end, if you want luxury, the Italians lead the way.

Four, even the dinkiest bathrooms have bidets. Beyond speaking a different language, it's the one thing that is really different than the US. It's possible to read twenty things online about bidets and still be uncertain how to use one. In trying to be delicate, most instructions are simply vague. Not here. To launch right into one of the most common questions, here are a few words about bidets: most of them work like little bubblers; adjust the stream until it's high enough to reach your parts when you straddle the unit with thighs touching the porcelain. Italians drop their pants to their knees, but for newbie Americans, slide those pants off entirely until you have figured out how to do this without getting them wet. Relax, reposition forward and back, give it a half a minute at least. Two tips: one, run the water until the warm water comes up. Two, bidets don't flush, so when you use toilet paper to dry off, remember to toss it into the regular toilet, not the bidet. The idea is to just flush the area hands-free for a while, no rubbing or soap.

Bidets have another purpose, and for that a little stool is provided in the bathroom. Bidets can be used to wash the feet, because those get stinky also. If there isn't a little stool, put the lid of the toilet down and sit on that.

By washing your privates and feet, and giving your underarms a wipe with a washcloth, the idea is you won't need to take as many showers, saving water.

There are a couple of other cultural differences . . . .

One, they don't have the American compulsion to fix up their buildings. Curb appeal here comes from looking old, not from looking like-new. They're proud of it. If the plaster falls off the stucco wall, doesn't mean anything needs to be done other than sweep it up. For the next 50 years. There are window shutters that are 200 years old, and look it. The current owner doesn't want to end their long run on his watch. The outside condition of the building tells you nothing about the care they take inside or the wealth of the family. In that regard they are more like the Chinese, who have a tradition of flat, plain walls facing outside to make it impossible to tell the actual wealth inside.

Two, there are no Walgreens. All their stores are crowded little shops that specialize in one thing. The reason there are so many Profumeria, which from the street can appear to sell only perfume, is because this is where to buy soap, hand lotion, lipstick, makeup, sunscreen, deodorant, shampoo, hair spray and hair supplies.

Three, what they consider chocolate is pathetic. Don't bother with anything labeled chocolate in Italy, go right for the fruit flavors or spice flavors, which are delectable. Filling up on something brown because you bought it so now you feel obligated to eat it, when you could be eating something of exquisite taste, is a lost opportunity.

Four, the ground floor is not the first floor; the first floor is what we call the second or even third, if there's a dining or event room level. So when she tells you that you're only on the second floor, be prepared for three flights of stairs.

Five, pharmacies have a green cross outside, which is often the only neon lighting on the outside of buildings.

They sell only prescriptions and certain other medications; you can't even buy a cough drop there.

In Italy, their idea of good-looking and
not needing repair is different than ours.
This is a B&B.

There is no bad pizza in Naples. It tastes twice as good as it looks.

Six, there is no bad pizza in Naples. Some are better... but all of them would be in the top 10% in the US. If you like the toppings, you'll like the pizza.

Seven, buy earrings from street vendors. I spent twenty minutes picking out a pair, only to find they were €1. The nicer ones were €2, but still. I should have spent three minutes and bought all the ones I liked.

Eight, Italy has a history of graffiti going back 4,000 years. Heck, they invented the word. It isn't that they like or have strong feelings about posters glued to walls, handwriting, and the like; it's simply always been like that. When it is on 2,500 year old wall fragments in a museum it's a national treasure, and when it's everywhere you look, it's part of the charm.

Nine, Nudity. Most people arrive in Italy not fore-warned, because mentioning it ruins frequent travelers' worldly façade. Statues, paintings, the top of door arches, on bowls, on chairs, floor tiles, you name it, naked men are all over. Not just items made 200 years ago, but 600 years ago and 1,500 years ago and 2,500 years ago. Naked men out-number naked women 5:1, a ratio that goes back as far as art itself in Italy.

Americans are used to nudes being women and men being, um, more shy than women about nudity in public. In Italy, men are not more shy. You see every last hair and wrinkle, and not stylized either. Larger than life and ten steps from the ice cream store.

The American reticence to having a good chuckle about it, in my humble opinion, is because they credit it to the artist's homosexuality. I'm not buying it. It went on for too long. Everybody had these statues in their garden and painted on their walls. I think it is exactly what it looks like: it's hot, men are the boss and when it's hot they don't want to wear clothes, end of story. Women, on the other hand, do up their hair, wear jewelry and don their most attractive dress in their statues and wall paintings. I get that. It's what I would do. There is no evidence that statues were commissioned by only gay men and sculpted by gay men for 2,500 years; it's a preposterous concept. I think the artwork reflected how people dressed. Most statues and wall paintings were vanity pieces, their version of photoshopping their head onto a great body.

There are naked people all over the Vatican because our bodies are God's work. Clothes are people's work. You hear it today, when people say "My body is my temple" and mean they take care of themselves. It's for a greater purpose, not vanity. It shows respect for the deity to be a responsible caretaker of the body he bestowed. The artwork is for the glory of God.

Children in Italy: the Italians stopped having them. Well, no, not entirely, but they have the highest average age of any country in Europe, meaning the least children. Don't expect much accommodation for children in Italy. Hotel rooms won't be child-proofed. Children can and are taken to Italy, but the experience is quite wasted on children under 13. This isn't DisneyWorld.

Small children simply cannot muster up several hours a day of awe at decorated ceilings, really good paintings, and lovely tile floors. The absolutely-everywhere naked men will raise questions that you will have to answer in a crowd, so prepare your answers. Within the Vatican you are almost never out of eyeshot of a male wee-wee. It's not just nudity—in every big city there are enticing Murano glass shops that you'll have to cut a wide berth with a seven year old in tow. Children have even less enthusiasm for purse and belt shopping and cannot be expected to share your delight with how good the house wine is. All they want are the balls sold by unsavory-looking street vendors (who sell nothing but balls) and to climb on things. Your fun is in inverse proportion to their fun, and vice versa.

Lovely tile floor in the Vatican

A trip to Italy can be tailored to be fun for children, but advice for that is in someone else's book. I've heard there are tours designed for grandparents/ grandchildren, and they're probably wonderful. Those folks will have vetted the sights, hotels and rest-aurants for safety and familiarity.

In general, the pre-ferences of grandparents and grandchildren are closer to-gether than those of kids and parents. For instance, parents want to go out drinking after 9 PM; grandparents want to eat around 6 PM and be back at the hotel by 9 PM; so do kids. Grandparents want to ride in boats and see light shows at sunset; so do kids. Parent-age adults want to see adult entertainment (the minimal clothing and racy joke kind) and drink in bars until midnight on their vacations. They want the house wine and spicy food. Grandparents want to eat something familiar, then watch the street performer and his trained cats do tricks. So do kids. Here's a thought: you and your spouse go to Italy, and use their airfare money to fund a Grandparent taking the kids to DisneyWorld.

Art. Everywhere you look, Italy has art, art, art.

All travel is worthwhile. Travel inoculates you with perspective. Perspective comes in handy later on. There may be a lot of reasons to talk yourself out of travelling, but never because it might be self-indulgent or frivolous. Travel to other countries provides a pivot point. The value of your opinions will forever be enhanced, because you have visited people on the other side of the ocean, and it shed light on what is the same and what can be different.

For instance, in Italy a tour guide provided a significantly different take on some events in World War II. My first thought was that the tour guide needs to read the history book. Then I immediately backpedaled from that conclusion. There is much truth in the saying "The victor writes the history." I'm going to ponder this juicy little conundrum of the conflicting tales. I'm leaning toward their version being right, since they live there. Could it simply be self-serving? You bet. And so could ours. Long ago I conceded that American journalists, always under deadline pressure, often using badly scribbled notes and motivated to spin the thing to make it more interesting, do not always record all the available details. Brevity and not recording every detail is their motto; they're in the business of making it more palatable, of 'organizing' it. History written by journalists is very clean, and often the light-grey hats get white while the dusky hats become black. But real life is messy, and in war everyone has some mud on them.

It might sound like I'm getting political, but I'm not. WWII was here. Be aware that you will bump into it. Brace yourself so you don't snort or laugh out loud when their history sounds different than the one you're familiar with. Maybe theirs is right, maybe ours is—you are on vacation and you can't tell, and it's not your job to set them straight. Let it roll like water off a duck's back. Or make a mental note to look into it later. A different history is also true of Germany, Austria, France, a lot of places. Perhaps everywhere.

~ ~ ~

The more you travel, the easier it gets. If you haven't traveled to Europe, or your travel in the US tends to be to relatives' homes or the same vacation spot, I'm not going to mislead you; this trip will be draining and stressful. But it will be fun, exciting, brave, fulfilling, and worth it. Your next trip will be half the stress—as long as you don't put years between trips. If you travel enough, you may even gain that distant, half-attentive look of the business travelers.

If you're squeamish about being a solo traveler, don't be. Italy is full of them, and you're allowed to make up an exotic back story for yourself without the least guilt. You can be meeting your fiancé, or having a fling with your boss but can never be seen together in public, or like the one I used, writing a travel book. Unfortunately, I got so suckered into my cover story that, well, here's the book.

Embrace The Adventure

The truth about travel is there's the trip we plan, and then there's The Adventure. The adventure is anything we didn't plan. The trip that goes according to plan is nice and we have a wonderful time. But what really makes for interesting conversation is The Adventure. If you have an adventure, you'll find it is the wellspring of 50% of all your sharing about the trip in the coming years.

The Adventure may not be apparent the moment it starts to happen. It could hide under the cloak of 'what do you mean it's closed?' or 'why didn't I know about this earlier' or 'my vacation is ruined.' However, if you brace yourself to recognize "Oh! My adventure is starting!" you will handle whatever comes in a better frame of mind and embrace the details so you can tell a more enthralling story later.

Dwight D. Eisenhower said about war: "Plans are worthless. Planning is essential." This is so-o-o-o true about travel also. Planning is about poking through all the options available, weighing them, making judgment calls based on skimpy or incomplete information, and coming up with a plan. The value of this background work becomes obvious when that incomplete information gets fleshed out in real time. It enables you to react quicker and make a better Plan B on the spot.

If you did some planning by looking at maps and floorplans, when you arrive at what you thought was the museum's main entrance and it is not the kind of busy it should be, it will dawn on you that the opening on the other side must be the real main entrance and hup-hup over there in time for the tour. If you didn't glance at any maps, as far as you know this is the only door and it will seem pretty risky to wander away.

In Italy, brochures, emailed instructions, and signage at the site will be skimpy and even misleading. It can seem like every Italian employee in the tourist business is put out having to tell you that tickets are bought a-a-a-all the way across the plaza, not at the door of the museum, or the line you spent twenty minutes in is for the blue ticket, not your green ticket whose line is over there. My thought, about four times a day was, 'Simply make a sign with an arrow and be done with being asked the same question 15 times a day.'

You may be told to 'follow the arrows' or 'turn at the sign that says XYZ' but there will be no such thing. There probably once was a sign but it fell down last year. The locals are still giving instructions as if it were there. When this happened to me I looped back to inform them, kindly, that the sign was no longer there, and they were mad at me, as if I'd torn it down.

Follow instructions within reason; if they point in this direction and you've gone two blocks with still no sight of it, ask another person. You may be on the right track. But be aware, all over the world there are people who give directions when they really don't know just to get you out of their hair, and then there are those who amuse themselves by messing with you. When you solicit assistance from passersby or workers, if you feel the least twinge about it, simply walk sixty feet and ask someone else. Sometimes the truth materializes as a compilation of four opinions.

If you are using maps, not GPS, you will find the street addresses in the large cities can be useless. This is because most major attractions either have a little spit of road devoted to them or are located in a plaza. Even though these attractions are nearly always in sight of or on a main roadway, travel books and tourist brochures persist in using the spit-of-road address that is too short to EVER show up on a map and cab drivers don't recognize, instead of an address on the main drag which would render it findable in 5 seconds. As for the plaza, there is literally no way to find a plaza except by tediously reading every word on the map. The famous travel guide books could, if they wanted to, provide an address on the nearest main drag, within eyeshot of the attraction, but they don't.

You can manually fix this. When you have some free time at home several days before you leave, use Google maps to search all the museums, restaurants, fountains and churches you definitely or maybe might see, zoom in to see the nearest main street and grab the address of some establishment on that street which is within eyeshot of the place, or two blocks straight west, or whatever is the case. Write these down. A tiny written list of addresses could save you half an hour a day of map-searching in Rome or Florence. Won't help in Venice, but that's another story.

Much of the advice here enables you to be resourceful. Plans are worthless, planning is essential. When things went wrong for you, planning gives you options. Plan enough, and even though ten things go wrong, you recover on the spot.

Here's a list of things that went wrong for me in Italy, but didn't really dent the trip:

- Twice I couldn't find a poorly-marked hotel. Once I asked a passerby by showing her the Italian name in my phone's calendar listing, and the other I had a screen-shot street view from Google in a printout, and was able to spot the ground-floor restaurant, where the staff pointed out the door.

- A phone software upgrade on my phone a few days before the trip left my calendar events intact, but ate all the notes and screenshots under each one, which I didn't discover until after landing. I had paper printouts of addresses, confirmation numbers, nearby good restaurants, meeting locations for tours, and so on in my luggage.

- An ATM ate my ATM card the second day (I left it hanging in there too long). I switched to cash advances.

- The Rome Hop-on, hop-off bus company was on strike. I took the subway or walked to the stuff I wanted to see.

- Two million people descended upon the Vatican and shut down most of the street traffic on the day I had to get to the train station across town. Subway again.

- In Venice, my route from train to hotel was flooded. All the books and reviews said it wouldn't happen this time of year. I rolled up my pants, fished out my flip-flops and waded through.

- In Naples/Pompeii I developed huge blisters on both heels. I cut holes in several layers of foam tape that I plastered around the blisters and scarcely felt them. I made no change or compromise to my daily schedule.
- In Florence, I never found my English-speaking tour group outside a palace. My paper receipt enabled me to get a ticket at the window, and ten minutes after I was in, unbelievably, I bumped into them.

Perfection is not the goal. Touching your bases with peace of mind and a possibility of enjoyment is the goal.

Anticipation and the Trip

It can feel spontaneous and fun to catch the soonest possible flight, but doing so could rob you of the greater portion of enjoyment: the anticipation. There are two phases to every trip: the anticipation, and the actual event. On reflection afterward, often the anticipation is the more enjoyable part.

If enjoyment had weight like grains of sand, anticipation's happy feelings may outweigh those occurring during the vacation. The vacation itself can be marred by sore feet, interrupted sleep, anxiety about travel connections, blocked views, quarrels between traveling companions, the food not agreeing with you, and rain. But the anticipation is pure pleasure. Later on, memory fixes the vacation to better match the anticipation. In memory you enjoy camaraderie with your travel companions and savor the scenery in pure gladness. Even if you didn't really at the time.

This is why my biggest piece of advice is to garner as much anticipation as you can for any trip by setting the date as far ahead as is practical. Selecting the dates months ahead also enables lower costs for airfare, a better selection of hotels, and availability of any tour or ticket you wish. Three weeks ahead, not so much. But it's always worth going, even on short notice. Go. There are bridges and statues and shopping and stunning views that are ticket-free. And there's the food. That is reason enough.

Old information can do more harm than no information. Whether it is advice on how the trains work or good restaurants, five-year-old information will steer you wrong. Old advice on airline rules, tour and museum costs, entrances and procedures could ruin your day.

Double-check the open hours of the venue on their specific website. Some websites will sell you tickets for a day of the week that the museum or event is closed. Museums stagger their closed days. Don't assume it's Monday, look it up. When in Rome, what the Pope is doing can have a big impact on your travel plans.

Don't be overly daunted when you open an Italian website and it's written in Italian. Most Italian tourist attractions have a button or a field, usually near the top, to select English. Even if they don't, use Google translate:

http://translate.google.com/

Click one of them to English and the other to Italian,

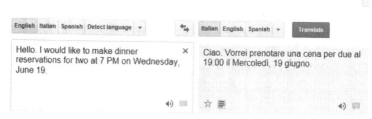

Look Mom, I can write Italian.

and either start typing, or copy-paste the website text into the Italian field to see what appears in English.

Some international websites have a nice feature that notices what language is predominant in your vicinity and shows you the website in your language. The downside of that is when you are on Wi-Fi in Italy, your regular shortcuts that you use all the time may bring up your favorite websites in Italian. If you can't seem to find your way to the English language version, there's always Google Translate to help you muddle through.

Ceiling decoration in the Vatican. There are dozens more like it, some considered better than this.

One of the best uses of Google translate is to check out the hotel and restaurant reviews that are written in Italian. Just copy-paste them in. There are certainly translation errors, but you can get the gist of it.

View from the top of the Colosseum in Rome. All over, the range in building age is huge. Within one block, structures 100 years old mingle with 500 year old and even 1800 year old buildings or parts of buildings.
Most buildings are repurposed every eighty years or so.

GETTING STARTED

Package Tour or Self-planned?

If you don't know what you want to do but just want to 'see Italy,' then you and your traveling companion can visit a travel agent and sign up for a package tour.

If you have a busy life so can't do much language-learning or studying of things worth seeing before the trip, then a package tour is what you should do.

If there are two of you and you both don't mind getting up early in the morning and you both hate planning and standing in lines, then a package tour is the right choice.

A travel agent, if you have a good one, will ask about the kinds of things you like, for instance, antiquities, art, stunning rural views or shopping; how much you want to cram into each day; how many days you can devote to the trip; then he or she will evaluate your energy level and stamina to match you up with an appropriate package tour. They save you hours of research in just knowing all the tour companies.

Tour companies come in high, medium, and economy levels. A quick Google of 'Italy tour packages' lets you peek before visiting the travel agent. There are ocean and river cruise tours.

Tours require even numbers: two, four or six people. Solo travelers pay double the 'each' price. On the other hand, most hotels in Italy have specific rooms for solo travelers that cost about two-thirds the price of a room for two, so financial reasons are compelling for the solo traveler to self-plan.

If you decide to self-plan, a great way to start is to study up on where the group tours go and what they see, even down to the day-by-day if you can, and duplicate the parts you like on your trip.

~ ~ ~

While travelogues, tourist books, and PBS shows have beautiful shot staging, are interesting and engaging, I warn that they can lead you seriously wrong, wrong, wrong. I think they start out meaning well, to be of help to travelers. As those media folks travel more and more, they seek out off-beat sights because they get jaded. The world-famous, breath-taking sites are old hat to them. Conversely, some become weary of the constant newness and extol the charm of drinking a beer on a "quaint" (read: poorly-maintained) small-town front porch while the sun sets. You can do that at home.

See *Picking What to See* chapter for more on this topic. At this point I'll just say, if you were to take their advice for your precious seven days in Italy and spend it visiting un-memorable locales, staying in seedy suburban walk-ups, eating raw food and staring at farmland, that would be missing the best of Italy in every regard. Seeing the Vatican, the Pantheon, the David statue in Florence, San Marco in Venice, antiquities in Naples, or dozens of other memorable sites is the goal of the first trip. Eating the food, the bakery, and the wine increases understanding. Save the relaxing rural vistas for future visits, when they add new dimensions to your Italy experience without supplanting Italy's one of a kind experiences.

While this is not true everywhere, going off the beaten path to meet the natives will only make the point that modern countries are more homogenous than ever before. Putting aside speaking a different language, they watch the same TV shows and movies, wear the same clothes, read the same news, play the same games on the internet, eat the same foods and drive foreign cars just like everybody you know. Indoor plumbing has been a thing here for 2,500 years. In the US, perhaps three generations tops. Italian inventors were big players in the development of electricity and the infrastructure we enjoy today. There are no natives here; just the inventors of civilization.

When you go to Italy, go to see all the sights everyone goes there to see. And for a good reason; they're absolutely unique.

Later, on your fifth or sixth visit to Italy, do a few days of those less touristy things. But never on your first or second trip. Trying to fast forward past the basics, being too worldly to visit a touristy site means remaining provincial, never becoming truly worldly.

Another food for thought, this one just my opinion, so filter it for yourself to see if it makes sense: when traveling overseas, staying at four or five star hotels or obtaining the top luxury tours insulates you against really experiencing the country you are visiting. You'll stay at American-style hotels just like those found in Milwaukee, eat food deliberately designed to cater to American tastes, and view the cities from air-conditioned cushy seats through tinted windows. There's nothing wrong with it, except . . . why travel 4,000 miles for that? How much nicer to save that for the third or fourth trip, after you have earned your 'worldly' status and can treat yourself to a little insulation from the mean streets of Rome.

View of excavated Pompeii. In many ways, the stores, the food, the art and the sense of humor have changed little in 2,000 years.

Packaged Tour Pros and Cons

Pros:

The hotels are nicer for the buck than individuals can negotiate.

The hotel knows what side its bread is buttered on, so hotel hassles are infrequent.

If you are a busy person and want a vacation that expands your experience, want to see the sights everyone talks about but don't have the time to research and book every single day ahead of time, plus can schedule the vacation days to fit the tour, then the packaged tour is made for you.

The trouble-shooting has been done. The routes and times have been worked out. Underestimating travel times, wait times or not understanding the entry requirements won't happen.

No standing in long lines for entry to the attractions or waiting for transportation.

Less stress.

Sleeping on the bus is possible and often done.

Tour guide speaks the language and is highly motivated to iron out any misunderstandings you cause.

Baggage-handling may be included, meaning very little heave-ho for you.

Between hotels, bags are kept safe on the bus or boat.

Tour guide can warn you or make suggestions based on experiences with a thousand previous travelers.

Events and side tours are chosen because they are wonderful experiences.

You can make friends with other travelers in your group that develop casually and might last a lifetime.

You don't need to study the customs, the story behind the landmarks or even the route ahead of time; all will be told to you as the moment arises.

There will be less strangeness; the tour arranges to sidestep disconcerting things to American eyes. Those things aren't what you came to see anyway.

There are tours aimed at special groups or interests, such as grandparent-grandchild tours, medieval focus tours or relaxing rural tours that are better than any one individual, with one shot to do it right, could manage.

Breakfast will be more like you're used to in the States and fairly consistent day-to-day regardless of country; with the swirl of new experiences on this trip, starting each day with a good breakfast is comforting.

Tour groups can develop great camaraderie, fit more into a day than solo travelers, usually walk right into attractions having huge lines, and may include non-American English speakers. Photo taken in Switzerland.

You're going through it with other English-speaking travelers, which could include New Zealanders, Australians, South Africans, British or Canadians, adding additional depth to the experience.

Cons

The pressure to buy their pricey trip insurance using scare tactics framed as 'happening often' can be outrageous. Their insistence that they will treat you disgracefully and shabby if you don't buy the insurance can leave a bad taste in the mouth about giving them your business.

The tour can require use of an airline that is inconvenient for you, adding hours to the trip or leaving from a farther away airport.

The tour will eagerly book you on a tour days or a few weeks from now, but that could mean only undesirable flight times and seats on the plane, not to mention unexpected additional flight costs which could be hundreds of dollars.

It's easy for the travel agent to have confidently told you dead wrong information, because what she said may be true of another tour, not this one. Keeping the fine points of ninety tour offerings straight in her head, when they are nowhere written, is a lot to ask.

You travel as a herd everywhere. Including restroom stops.

Early morning starts every day require being packed up with breakfast done by 8 AM, which can mean a 5:30 AM alarm time for the first one to use the bathroom. (there's napping on the bus, though)

Baggage weight and amount limits that may not match the airline's.

Hotel breakfast buffets are lacking in local foods; a good opportunity for tasting local cuisine is wasted.

Two to a room is a good deal financially but for a solo person the cost is almost doubled.

There are very few chances to go off to see something not on the tour.

Hotels are mostly on the fringe of the city, not in the heart. This is a very mild 'con', though, because you get to see two kinds of locales, big city and small town living, plus it will feel safer and the room can be more spacious.

If someone in the group rubs you the wrong way or the guide is hard to understand, you're stuck.

Brochures are deliberately misleading or vague, making assessing what is an extra side trip or upgrade and what is included difficult.

Shopping time is often brief.

The tour guide may make most of his money from side trips and workshop visits (glass-blowing, diamond-cutting, wooden shoe-making, and so on) where he gets a percentage of the purchases from the business owner. These are often a good show, but the expectation to buy something at the end can be uncomfortable.

At the end of the trip the tour guide may give you an opportunity to give him a tip, which to be fair he or she may have earned. However, you might be low on Euros, and using the ATM for a very small withdrawal incurs disproportional fees.

You're on your own for the flight to and from your first and last destination, which can be in different cities. Getting boarding passes, meeting baggage requirements and making your transfers is all on you, and you are responsible for meeting the airlines checked bag and carry-on bag rules, navigating the airport, along with leaving enough time for standing in lines, having proper ID, customs, baggage scans, long hallways, and choosing ground transportation to and from the hotel.

Self-Arranged Tour Pros and Cons

Pros

Economical to travel as a solo person; European hotels have low-cost single-bed rooms for you.

Can eat when, where and what you want.

Can choose how long to stay in each city depending on your interests and the amount of things you want to see.

Can visit a collection of sites and places that no packaged tour encompasses.

Delightful anticipation in web-searching to pick hotels, tours, tickets, and sights to see weeks ahead.

You can pick the airline, airport and flight times you prefer.

You can schedule sleep-in days, where you don't get up until 8 AM or later, if your idea of a vacation is no alarm clock.

You can do a mix of hotels and bed and breakfasts, for a different view of the country

Flight can be booked very early, before any other costs are incurred, when seat choice is excellent.

Cost can be spread out over several months.

You never have to bear museums or tours or even cities you don't care to see.

You can time the trip to exactly catch an event or ceremony in a certain city that is hugely meaningful to you, such as Tour de France in France, the Pope conducting Mass in Rome, or a performance event.

It can include everything you want and nothing that you don't want.

Cons

You're on your own for the flight to and from your destination, but you had no expectation of help with that.

Most hotels will hold your bags securely after you check out (verify this is a bullet point feature on the hotel's website) but it means you have to hike back to the hotel before going to the train, bus station or airport.

You'll need to learn a couple of phrases in their language ahead of time.

When you run into trouble or confusion, approaching strangers with "Mi scusi, parli inglese?" or the equivalent will be necessary.

Money can't buy help schlepping your bags around; unless you bring your own servant for this, count on carrying them up and down steps many times.

Lots of hours spent reading reviews, considering Top Ten lists and studying street maps picking out hotels, tours, tickets and sights to see. (I love this part, but not everyone does)

It's up to you to ferret out whether events, holidays or ceremonies will block streets, change schedules or affect transportation, and bend your plans around them.

Museums in a city often stagger their closed days; don't schedule one for Tuesday without really checking if it's open.

Only a compulsive attention to dates and times, triple-checking and more, will suffice when buying train tickets, guided tours, reserving hotels and the like. Choosing the wrong date because the online calendar starts with Monday, not Sunday, or forgetting 06-07-14 is July 6, not June 7, outside of the US is a common reason for snafus.

If you don't buy tickets online a few weeks ahead, hours of your trip may be spent in boring lines.

No tour guide to help you handle any trouble you might get into.

It's difficult to develop a reasonable schedule for a place you haven't been.

Only map-studying will tell you if you can walk, or if not, what kind of transportation will get you between locations and how long it will take.

Transportation choices: it takes effort to pick the least stressful, least-time and least-expense mode based on your destinations. Renting a car often isn't it.

Your experience is confined to choices made before you leave home; it's hard to tell what will feel most worthwhile. Not deciding until you arrive curtails choices even more, plus adds pointless hours of waiting to the mix.

You will be more aware of what you missed seeing than the packaged tour folks, who may leave a country after six days honestly thinking they saw all the good stuff.

Cruise trip Pros and Cons

Pros

For the most part you unpack once, then visit multiple destinations yet sleep in the same bed

The heart of the city is often right there when you disembark, just as convenient as pricey city hotels you could never afford.

The level of amenities on board and luxury in food and entertainment is excellent for the price

There's so much to do while traveling on the ship that getting off in the cities visited may not be that compelling.

For people who want a relaxing, social and not intense vacation, this is the thing to do

Cons

The rooms are small. Efficient, with space intelligently used, but compact.

Seasickness.

Rigid return-to-ship times make people limit how far from the ship they're willing to go

There are a lot of unplanned costs that the first-time cruise passenger didn't budget for

Tipping the staff is often expected, and being a large tipper early in the cruise is a way to ensure good service for the remainder

For winter trips to warmer climates it's a good idea to book a flight two days ahead of departure and stay at a local hotel, just in case snow days anywhere in the US backs up flights for a day.

Bundling of cruise, hotel stay and flight may cost extra for the convenience; find out the cost of the cruise alone to check out if booking the flight and hotel yourself could be cheaper.

Travel insurance

Travel insurance can increase the cost of a trip up to 20%, and the odds are good that even if you make a claim it will not pay you back as much as it cost you.

The saddest travel tales of woe are heard from people who bought trip insurance and still lost their money, plus the insurance cost. The insurance didn't cover their reason, or they missed the deadline, or the amount recompensed still left them several hundred out of pocket.

Travel insurance is one of the fastest-growing scams today. Once upon a time it was real and useful, and cost about 2% of the trip value. What we have today has the same name, but it is an entirely different animal.

My view on trip insurance is the same as my view on the extended warranty: with the money I save on not buying it, I mentally create a pool I can tap when needed. But I travel a lot.

Cruises and group tours: I do not have first-hand experience, but I hear that cruise and tour companies lay on the veiled threats so thickly about how risky it is to skip their insurance that I recommend you simply add the cost + trip insurance and consider that the real cost of the trip. It's not an optional cost, it's simply part of the true cost of cruises and package tours. Normal customer service has been moved to another bucket with a pricetag. Omit at your peril. They promise to treat you shabbily if you decline, and I bet they will.

Contracts. I provide more information on vetting a contract in my book "Negotiating When Money Matters," but one thing that is useful to know about contracts, especially travel insurance contracts, is: *none of the verbal statements need to be binding or true.*

Whatever anyone tells you is in the contract is absolutely meaningless unless you see it in hard text with your own eyes. Have the speaker point to it in the contract. It could even be written in the contract, but then in another section of the contract the applicability of that section could be removed. Anecdotal evidence, which is all I've got, is that a significant amount of the time they squiggle out of covering claimants, or pay out less than the claimant paid for the insurance.

Last minute cancellations are almost never covered. Why? When you inform the trip insurance firm of a cancellation a week ahead, the travel-savvy people at the insurance company get on the phone and call in cancellations with each entity, meaning no charge. With a big flourish they give you money, but only the exact same money you could get if you made those calls or emails yourself. A deductible covers the money they can't get refunded, so their 'insurance' seldom pays out more than the customer could manage themselves.

Most of the usual reasons for postponing trips are not covered.

If you're cancelling a trip more than a week ahead and do not have trip insurance, taking the old 'begging and pleading' route works. An apologetic tone and earnest goodwill can often make a hotel permit a date change, and for $75 or so the airline will allow you to apply the ticket cost to a different flight in the next year. With a lot of phone calls in a pleasant, remorseful tone (enlist a friend or relative with a good voice if this is not you), the financial damage due to cancelling a trip can be mitigated decently.

Not to belabor a point, but heck yes, to belabor it, do not take 'non-refundable' or 'not changable' at face value, ever. Always go for it and ask nicely. Always share a good-sounding sob story—especially if the real reason is weak. Always express profound regret, call yourself an idiot for being in this position, whatever self-effacing approach meets the needs of the person on the other end who can say yes as easily as say no.

I am not speaking of Italy alone with this advice, but am encompassing the whole world. Speaking of situations that come up more than eight days prior to the trip, 59 times out of 60 it is no skin off their nose to allow you to move your visit two months or even twelve months, or allow you to give it to someone else (read: sell on Craigslist).

It takes more finesse within 48 hours. Still, the tourist business would rather retain a customer and get good word of mouth than keep your money but risk something nasty on TripAdvisor that turns away six other customers. Your strongest tool is a hint that you like writing reviews ... so it's a good idea to be accommodating with you.

You yourself can mitigate trip cancellation damage at any stage, even within 48 hours by expending some effort on the phone. Calling even one hour before the event can mean getting your money back, because by then your trip insurance may have abandoned you. That venue might be sold out and turning away walk-ups; it could be no loss to let you cancel as long as you call before, not after. Even ten or fifteen minutes before can make all the difference.

I can't say it too strongly: the seller of travel insurance can and will tell you verbally that you are covered for cancellations up to the last minute or for unexpected expenses or losses during the trip. It's legal to lie to you verbally. They may blurt out anything or promise anything about it, either before or after you sign. It is entirely your responsibility to read the contract and if a verbal statement you are counting upon isn't in there, you can add it in pen to the margin and both parties initial and date the edit. You may cross out what you don't like, also to be initialed and dated by both parties.

Contracts are a meeting of the minds, and your mind counts. Don't sign anything you don't agree with or has key promises missing.

The allowed reasons for trip cancellation are always rather narrow. Your best friend getting in a bad car accident is not going to cut it; neither is a kitchen fire the day before the trip. Getting arrested for overdue parking tickets is ineligible. Your dog needing to go to the vet won't qualify.

If you want travel insurance, call your homeowners or renters insurance company and give them first dibs. They often have a short-term rider you can activate. The odds are much better they will handle claims in a workmanlike fashion and get a check to you in a decent amount of time.

Second choice is to do your research and obtain travel insurance from a reputable company that doesn't have skin in the game. You want insurance from insurance people, not an extra charge by travel people.

Credit cards have free travel insurance. Not all, so check your benefits brochure. Their coverage may look good, but be aware there are a lot of qualifying details that have to align. Most of the cards that offer it require all the pre-charges for the trip be on their card: hotel, flight, trains, etc. If they find you put something on a different card (how would they find out? Who knows, but it's a risk), then you aren't covered. Some may provide free flight cancellation reimbursement up to $2,500, but for only covered events involving you or a select few immediate family members.

They may have trip delay insurance and extended lost-baggage coverage, covering more than the airlines' dinky amount. These are actually meaningful, and free if you used that card to buy the flight. All of their coverage is additive, meaning starts only after other coverage has maxed out.

Say the airline lost your checked bag with belongings valued at $900. Suppose the airline covers $200 for lost bags, the trip insurance you bought covers to $500, and the credit card covers to $750. You will make three claims: the airline will give you $200, the trip insurance $300, and the credit card $250. Let the fun begin!

Travel Life Insurance. Many credit cards have travel life insurance, meaning your heirs get life insurance if you die in transit, often around $250,000. Your heirs have to claim it, and know which card you used, and it goes without saying you can't remind them the day after. It's something you actually have to say the day before you leave, "Now if my plane goes down, MasterCard has 250 big ones coming your way if you file a claim. Kiss-kiss. Love ya."

A lawyer suggests adding a line to your will that says something like, "in the event my death happened while I was traveling as a ticketed passenger, file a claim for travel accident insurance with the credit card company used to buy the ticket."

You may be able to achieve a level of travel insurance you feel comfortable with by using a good travel charge card and following their rules to the letter of the law. But the kitchen fire or trip to the vet will still never qualify.

The Phone and Staying in Touch

The cell phone is the Swiss Army Knife for travel today. I'm still amazed at how these have changed the world. Whether a tablet or phone, it can be a flashlight, compass, and notepad; it can store dozens of maps and books, translate the spoken or written word, keep your calendar, store your confirmation numbers, get email, and more. Some tourist sites have an audio tour you can download to your own device, using your own headset--do not forget to bring earphones or a headset!

Today's phones have better cameras than $400 could buy 15 years ago. My iPhone 5 took amazing photos in dim light, photos that twenty years ago would take forty seconds of practiced fussing with shutter speeds, not to mention the right film loaded into the camera in the first place. Many of my iPhone photos are in this book. Realistically, if you're going to use the photos for wallpaper on your personal computer, posting on Facebook, or emailing to friends, the dpi of your phone camera is plenty enough. Over 950 photos fit on my iPhone 5 with room to spare.

Even if you decide to keep it on airplane mode the entire trip and click 'roaming' to off, it is simply the handiest thing for traveling.

Phone or Tablet when Traveling

1) Things happen. Have paper backup of schedules, addresses, phone numbers, important stuff. Even four pages printed out and stashed in the suitcase can literally rescue your trip if your phone takes a header on the second day.

2) Those find-your-phone apps don't work like you expect overseas; guard that puppy well.

3) Theft of your phone or tablet is more likely than purse-snatching or wallet-lifting.

4) Obtain a compact portable power charger, under $20, for an extra eight hours of use or 24 hours standby.

5) Traveling without phone calls from home. Try it. People have done it for generations.

6) Program the weather button by city; it will update via Wi-Fi, and will always show the right time.

7) Charger: if it says 110-220V or 120-240V, it can be used in Italy with a $7 plug adapter; converter not needed.

8) Consider buying a phone and plan/minutes in Italy; with some US carriers, this is the cheapest way.

9) Phone + bathroom = disaster.

A phone can rack up charges EVEN when in airplane mode. Charges can be incurred when your calls go to voicemail, and could be over $5 a call. These fatuous rules could change tomorrow, but in the event this is still how your carrier gets you by the short hairs, go online before you leave and forward your calls to any US phone number that rings and rings, doesn't pick up, meaning has no voicemail or answering machine. Not a fax, because a fax actually picks up and proceeds to make a bad noise. An unplugged fax would work, as long as you can be sure no one will 'help' you by reconnecting it while you're gone.

Outgoing calls can be made with the phone up until you flip it into Airplane mode, but no incoming until you go online and discontinue the forwarding.

A phone on airplane mode will continue to show your hometown time, in my case EST Boston time the whole trip. That's a good thing. It kept the calendar faithful to the times I entered. A 9 AM tour start would have moved to 3 PM Italy time had the phone 'known' I changed time zones. Each event can be changed individually, or you can enter them all as dual time, but both of those are a pain in the neck. For local time I had the weather button.

Many people travel with their tablets. If you decide to do this, you won't look odd, you'll fit right in. It has a great camera with a huge viewfinder! If it's Wi-Fi only, there is no possibility of accidentally incurring phone charges. Keep the cell phone at home and there's no risk of voicemail charges either. A tablet weighs about as much as a water bottle. It is easy to view stored maps or read books. You can carry around a library.

Whether tablet or phone, when you're bored and waiting, you can read or play solitaire or Sudoku or other games that are playable in airplane mode. In the notes area, it will transcribe your spoken notes about the trip into text.

Word and Excel programs are free or just a few bucks. Before you leave home, copy-paste from the internet anything and everything that may pertain to your trip into a

Word doc, such as screenshots of hotel and tour confirmation pages, photos of how the restaurant looks from the street, bits of maps, parts of reviews, anything that catches your fancy. The day before you leave, copy the Word doc onto your phone. Later on you may have to hunt through the doc for it, but at least you know it's in there.

Just remember, having a weak moment and connecting to make even one call can result in data fees of several hundred dollars. All your other apps will immediately start updating (pulling ads) and the GPS will pull non-stop. Depending upon your carrier, using Skype on your phone could result in charges even if you are in a free Wi-Fi zone. Hotels may have a computer you can Skype from for free.

An overseas temporary plan costs over $100. Ask questions and be sharp, because they don't make it easy to understand. If you use your phone without it, charges could be over $1,000. It's obvious those charges are merely punitive, not reflecting actual costs to the carrier. Unless you want to devote the next two years of your life to a class action suit, if you decide you won't make any phone calls with your phone, stick to your guns. If the call you wish to make is local, consider asking a local if they might make it for you. Waiters, tour guides, friendly people usually say yes.

Even without being able to make calls, texts or use the GPS, your phone still has its calendar features, notes, voice memos, some of the apps, stored docs with maps, and of course the indispensable camera.

You cannot use GPS in airplane mode. Rather, you can use it but it won't have that pinpoint accuracy of finding where you are. When you have Wi-Fi, it will 'locate' you at the nearest tower—which is usually not that far off and renders a usable street map, but using the directions button may not be relevant to where you are sitting.

Don't count on plugging any addresses into Google Maps or Yelp and letting it guide you if you have not signed up for your carrier's Italy/European plan for the duration. If you do call to set it up, be sure you triple check that the service you're buying is for Italy.

Anecdotal stories abound regarding know-nothing phone duty staff who sign up first-time travelers for something that costs a pretty penny, but ends up not being calls-plus-data for Italy.

Perhaps it's the plan for some other country, or for the wrong timeframe, or your phone isn't GSM, it's CMDA (type of communication method with the towers) and Italy has only GSM.

GSM = what Italy has. AT&T uses this.

CMDA = what Verizon and some other US cell phone companies have, won't work

GSM/CMDA = dual mode phones, might work IF GSM is turned on and lots of other ifs.

Know-nothing phone answering people at your carrier might sell you something costing $150 for your overseas trip which doesn't render service once you get there. Just as bad, you might get service but find $400 in charges on your phone bill the next month because they didn't sell you what you intended to buy.

Plead your case all you like, I have not heard of anyone getting more than 20% knocked off when this happens. It might not happen to 90% of people signing up, but 70% of those are not first timers and they know the magic words, what to ask for, so they advise the carrier's staff what to do. My impression is the odds of a mistake happening to a first timer, unless you talk to at least two people at your service provider and insist they look it up, is fifty-fifty.

To belabor the point, I've heard tales that flipping off airplane mode for six minutes to make one call or use the GPS resulted in $200 in charges that couldn't be made to go away. To put it in perspective, as of this writing, Verizon charges $5 per Mb; an emailed photo could cost $30. Free apps with ads could download a mini video, costing you $50 a minute. Carriers are only interested in selling you an international data and calling package for hundreds of dollars before you leave. If you don't spend the money up front with them, the charges are merely punitive, not a realistic covering of the cost. Over $1,000 is likely.

When it comes to the phone being on, how much you use it doesn't matter; the GPS will be pulling data every ten seconds if not more, and even Solitaire may be downloading ads. Train your family members or co-workers to reach you by email or use What's App to text, which you'll view when it's convenient for you; for gosh sakes you're on vacation, the world can accommodate your needs a bit for once.

WhatsApp

To stay in touch if you keep the phone on airplane mode the whole trip, get the app "WhatsApp Messenger" by WhatsApp Inc. for your phone, available for Android and iPhone. It looks and feels like text messaging but is entirely Wi-Fi. In fact, if you exchange texts with only a handful of people, have them all load WhatsApp, enabling you to skip having a texting fee on your plan. This app can also send photos plus you can talk your messages into it if you don't like to type.

For doing serious typing, say emails or editing Word docs, consider bringing a lightweight Bluetooth keyboard weighing only a few ounces. A bonus is that the phone and keyboard fits on the smallish train tables and airplane trays with room to spare for the coffee cup and snack. Don't laugh. It is surprisingly not that hard to use a phone screen as a monitor. Old-timers, uh, I mean computer pioneers, cut their programming teeth on seven inch monitors just a shade bigger than today's phones.

~ ~ ~

Phone theft is the most lucrative kind of tourist theft happening today. The petty thieves have changed focus from wallets to phones, because phones are easy to convert to cash and the police don't care like they do with wallet thefts. You are more likely to have your phone stolen than your purse.

Say no to anyone who offers to snap a photo of you with your camera phone. It'll be gone. Don't set it down on ledges, on the restaurant table, or anywhere; pocket it between uses.

Picking What to See

Travel books for Italy and the individual cities are full of information, but are no help in selecting what to see and where to eat on a trip. Sounds impossible, but true. The maps are good, history facts are accurate, and everything they say was once true and may still be true.

Here's what you do: Online, there are webpages where the authors give their opinion for Three Days in Rome, Two Days in Venice, that sort of thing. Google those, they are a wonderful place to start. Visit those sites and you can't go wrong.

The itinerary from an established package tour also contains the sites worth seeing—to a point. There may be a couple of sites present only for financial reasons. One that comes instantly to mind is leaving Florence for a day trip to Pisa. No one who bused over to Pisa thought it was worth that amount of hours of their precious Italy time. The day would have been better spent in a museum or church in Florence. If you have less than four days in Florence, don't take the side trip to Pisa if you can avoid it. There's way too much good stuff in Florence.

Travel books provide detail-filled background for sites, statues, fountains, bridges, museums and churches, but that doesn't reveal whether they're worth seeing. Almost every street corner in Rome could have an impressive pedigree reaching back a thousand years; that doesn't mean it's worth going out of your way to visit.

In Italy more than most places, travel books can half-help you by getting you interested in certain sights, museum special tours, and the like, but when you arrive close to or at the location, that is when you find out they left out critical information like tricky access to the site, unexpected requirements like no one under twelve or no backpacks, and the really important details like what the tour is called in their language and where to pay for admission; those may be in a different building or offsite.

Travel books organize the information about a city by breaking it up into neighborhoods, then recommending restaurants, sights to see and hotels in each. When it covers a whole country, it breaks it up into discrete areas and devotes a fair slice of content to each area. The problem is, no one visits a city or country like that. We want to see the main stuff, period. We want clear advice on good hotels near sites on our itinerary and near transportation.

The truth is, some areas of town have forty wonderful restaurants while others have three, but the book dutifully lists four for each district; one district has nine famous destinations and another has one good one and two so-so ones, but the book lists three for each district.

The result of 'being fair' to all districts of each city or country is there is no telling what's really good. All restaurants in one district could be worse than the top twenty restaurants in another. This means a tourist could travel far to eat at a recommended restaurant in another district that is not half as good as the unlisted restaurant around the corner from the hotel. I'm speaking from personal experience on this.

In being fair to all districts, the writers have lost touch that most readers are using the book to figure out what's really worth seeing during a precious three or four days of their entire lives. Often, all the high points are in two districts. But you couldn't tell that from flipping through the book.

Some have tried to remedy that by tacking on a section that highlights the good stuff, but they get carried away there too and pack it with nine days' worth of sight-seeing.

Despite having a recent year slapped on the cover, most of them were written in the 1970s. Updating entails phoning for some price changes and swapping out a few photos. The world they describe is gone. Those restaurants don't serve those dishes anymore. That wing of the museum isn't open to the public anymore.

Travel books can be very wrong but have such air of authority that you never doubt. In the latest edition of the two most well-known travel guides, almost every paragraph about something I actually did or saw in Italy contained an incorrect statement. Example: one book says visitors climb the Vatican's spiral stair-case to get to the ticket window; actually, you already have your ticket and are embarked on the tour when you visit the staircase. It's not a big deal when one sees the staircase; it's the unreliability, the parallel universe that's not quite like ours that they are writing about.

One book said high water in Venice is a problem in the fall, but it is a problem in the spring. It talked about hotels stocking rubber boots for tourists, but they don't; everyone uses disposable light blue plastic leggings with a footpad, and I never saw a soul with high water boots on—not even old men. Time and again these books say Italians don't wear shorts. Maybe they didn't twenty years ago but they do now. The problem with shorts in Italy isn't about fitting in, it's that if you see a grand old church you wish to pop in to study the art and rest the ol' feet, they won't let you in with bare

Vatican spiral staircase; not a ramp to the ticket window

knees, peeking-out tummies and exposed shoulders.

As a tourist, you need to cover your knees even though the locals do not.

Museums in Travel books. They often list what's in a museum floor by floor, similar to someone telling you what's in each aisle at the grocery store. That doesn't help a cook develop a menu, and it doesn't help you plan your visit. I suppose the idea is that you will bring the book along and read it while in the museum; don't do that. Nearly all museums have audio tours that provide much more while keeping your eyes free to look.

Travel writers who advocate seeking out non-tourist locales and restaurants are deeply mistaken for first-timers, and even for second-time visitors to that country. Those things are by definition less popular. There's a reason why people come to see the main attractions; they are worth it.

When planning your own trip, you need to allow enough time between sites. Budget showing up an hour early for trains. Assume the wait for a bus is almost the full between-bus time. If you have a car, assume driving at half the speed limit and allow twenty minutes to find parking.

The irony of travel, just like project management, is that crowding things too tightly means you miss more. Instead of buffer time between events taking the shock, the next event is missed, and then the one after that.

Good planning means that a mistake may cost more money, but not a drastic change in touching the bases you want to touch. An easy way to do this is to stagger must-dos with nice-to-dos in between. If something goes amiss, say you miss the 8 AM tour time but they'll let you take the 10 AM tour, you can say Yes!!! because your next thing is after lunch.

Beautiful wall mosaic at Herculaneum, just north of Pompeii, which was covered by the same Mt. Vesuvius eruption. People liked keeping cool in the summer and weren't big on sewing. Everywhere you look, people Photoshopped their head onto the same handsome bodies.

*In Herculaneum, a 2,000 year old window ledge
whose design and symmetry are familiar today*

*An ordinary street in Rome. Window ledges are pretty
much the same. Note the trees are actually in the street.*

Picking Where to Eat

Travel books also do you a disservice in their choice of restaurants to feature; in hindsight, having taken their recommendation several times, I am left puzzled about what qualifies a restaurant to get prominently featured.

Here's what you do: eat where there are a lot of people enjoying themselves and the food leaving the kitchen looks good to you; that's never a mistake. Going to the less-busy travel-book-recommended restaurant and giving it a shot is a gamble, but gamblers don't always lose. They just lose most of the time.

Make reservations online ahead of time. It's the best way to get a table at the more popular restaurants during the busy season. In April to mid-June it's less busy. Italy is geared toward the peak months of July and August, so except for the very top restaurants, you can walk in most of the year and get a seat, save for perhaps two hours per day.

True story: at one restaurant for which I made mid-May reservations weeks in advance because the travel books said it was a favorite of tour groups and always full, I arrived at 6 PM and was the ONLY customer! My waiter was having his dinner at a table and wasn't zippy about getting up to serve me, finished most of it before coming over. I remained awkwardly the sole customer my whole meal. Between bouts of serving me, my waiter sat two tables down sipping his coffee in front of his dirty plates. The food was wonderful, the décor was as promised. But around the corner were bustling al fresco dining facilities with live music, and I was stuck here with Mr. Grumpy Waiter.

The big group: Traveling with siblings, cousins, parents and grandparents can be great fun, but when it comes to restaurants, the wait time increases exponentially. Really think hard about needing to all sit together for every meal. Perhaps just one meal a day, say the breakfast buffet at the hotel, will suffice. If you can break into two or three 4-person groups for lunch or dinner, you will save forty-five minutes per meal and see more of Italy. This works even better if some are vegetarian, diabetic, glucose-intolerant, under five or what have you; everyone doesn't have to march to their drummer every single meal.

If you decide before leaving that is how you are going to handle lunch and dinner, splitting up, it doesn't become an opinion or a statement about others in your party. It's just sticking to plan. Swap around who eats with who so everyone eats with everyone every two to three days. No hard feelings. PS: this means that mom doesn't always eat with her child; pull an oar, folks, give her a break.

Chocolate: We're accustomed to American chocolate, which is modeled after Belgian chocolate and Swiss chocolate. Don't make any special efforts for Italian chocolate, which is more of a hint 'o' chocolate to us. I found more happiness with what they do with vanilla and fruits. The Italians are masters at creme. If you think of the creamy delights they can manage with milk, just imagine when they set their hearts to using the heavier stuff.

Breakfast in Italy: One day I selected a restaurant for breakfast because it had lively signage promising an American breakfast, and I was still queasy from adventuresome eating the day before. My first thought upon receiving it was, 'close but no cigar.' The eggs were scrambled without milk, and scrambled was the only choice. The bacon was fried but refrigerator cold. The bread was sliced but not toasted and there was no butter. The potatoes were lumpy, not hash browns, and not fried in oil. No salt and pepper on the table. It was as if someone had seen an American breakfast from thirty feet away through a glass window and imitated it.

Italians don't have any use for butter. They serve bread without it. Some of the nicer restaurants have olive oil, but it does nothing to improve the basic dryness of the bread. Where Italy shines is in the little hard rolls. Sliced bread in Italy is an acquired taste; the hard rolls have that wonderful taste that develops the more you chew it.

Closer view of the Duomo in Florence. Like most major buildings in Italy, it has three or four names. It's also Il grande museo del Duomo, Basilica or Cattedrale Santa Maria del Fiore, and Duomo di Firenze. All the color comes from using different natural stone and marble. Artwork is mosaic tiles.
Construction began in 1296 and the dome was finished in 1436. The outer design we see today was not completed until 1887.

Picking Where to Stay

Hotels. For the same reasons as mentioned in What to See and Where to Eat, don't select hotels from travel books. Instead, zoom in on Google maps to the part of town you want to stay in, type 'hotel' in the address bar; bed and breakfasts will also show in the results. Then start vetting the choices in your price range on sites like tripadvisor.com and yelp.com. On vacation, location is 3/5ths of the value; $1/5^{th}$ is price and $1/5^{th}$ is service, maintenance, noise, etc. You want to know what travelers who were there last month are saying, not the travel book blurb that has not changed in five years.

So, first pick what you want to do, get a rough idea of what you want to be close to, and then select the hotel.

There are a lot of perfectly fine hotels in all price ranges in every city. A hotel is a means to an end, and the end is convenient access to your sight-seeing plans.

Getting your heart set on a certain hotel and bending your vacation plans around it is a waste. Think hard about overspending for a great view or other amenities. Are you coming to Italy to stay in your room and gaze out the window? Didn't think so. The good-view hotel is for your third or fourth visit, not your first.

With one exception: some hotels have a rooftop dining area with to-die-for views. If you're certain your schedule allows time to eat up there, then indulge. Put another way, the room with a view could easily run an extra $150, and if you force yourself you'll stand for ten minutes at the window. What else could you do for $150 that's more memorable?

The hotel can be either easy to get to when you arrive or leave, or otherwise be near an early-start tour so you can simply walk there. If you can't decide, pick the latter. When seeing the Vatican or David or the catacombs is a must-do for you, being within walking distance removes all kinds of variables.

Public transportation, major tourist-oriented companies and government employees have several strikes per year. By law these strikes are limited to three days. If one does happen while you're there, it's nice when your main event is a block away.

Bid websites. These are the sites where you enter the days you'll travel, the city, and perhaps a few other things like star rating you wish, and either must accept the lowest bidder or they impose other restrictions. These are fine for a mad-weekend or a visit to a city in the US that you've been before, but I cannot say too strongly, don't do this as a first-timer on something as important as this vacation. The location of your hotel and its good-fit to your situation will save you time and stress. The savings is likely to be a poor trade for the extra travel hours you incur.

Ask about construction. Ask how far your room is from the construction to see what they say. Renovations are often going on nearby, and the sooner you ask to be moved the more likely a different room will be available.

Courtyard view. You might get a room that faces a dinky inner courtyard. Don't sniff at these or be so quick to demand a room with a view.

For one, you didn't come to Italy to sit in your room staring out the window! If the bad view encourages you to step across the street for a pizza instead of ordering room service, it's done its job.

For two, that street view window goes both ways, and 90% of travelers find they draw the curtain as the sun sets so they aren't on display.

For three, the odds are the courtyard room is going to be quieter, more insulated from odd noises that wake you in the night. Not 100% of the time—courtyards can have noises too, especially if it rains—but most of the time. Getting some sleep is the main thing that prevents crankiness as the trip wears on.

Four, because the building is often repurposed to be a hotel now, the window having a view might be in a spot where it is not very comfortable to stand and soak in the view, much less sit. If you've been walking all day and are too tired and grandeured-out to stand before a window sucking up a view that under other circumstances would wow you, spending $50 extra for a good view might be a poor use of your money.

Most tourists will be out of the hotel room thirteen hours a day and when they're in it, be involved in washing, eating and sleeping, along with satisfying your curiosity about what they watch on TV and being amused by Bruce Willis speaking perfect Italian. Oh wait—that's me.

Hotels often have rooftop breakfast areas/evening wine bars. Utilizing the rooftop is far more common in Italy than in the US, and often this is really the only 'good' view the hotel has, due to how close other buildings are on all sides. Hotels will mention if they have a rooftop deck.

In hotels in Italy you can expect toilet paper, bath towels, a TV with remote control, windows that open, a view of a wall twenty feet away, some shelf or counter space for clothes, table and chair, overhead light, tile in the bathroom, pillow, sheets, wall hooks, bidet, and some level of breakfast or cappuccino provided.

Booking the room. All hotels worth staying at have an internet presence, but that doesn't mean they have their own website. Don't be surprised if you click to book a room and find yourself at Booking.com or another third party site. Keep your antenna up for something fishy; however, this is the usual way bed & breakfasts and smaller hotels book their rooms online.

Hotel Star Ratings

In Italy they do not mean what you think they mean, good, better, best. The rating a hotel advertises could be from one of several sources. Online booking sites have a ranking, and so does Forbes. For instance, a quite luxurious hotel with great views could get lower stars because the lobby is in a different building from some of the rooms.

In Italy, many hotels and all the B&B are repurposed buildings. This is part of the charm. Hotels under three stars could have very odd entrances, walking across courtyards, staircases that look like they used to lead to the servant's quarters, or you need to go out and around the corner to get to your room, etc. A hotel that has a couple of rooms in an adjacent building can never be four stars, no matter what else they do. Which means pricing is loosely tied to rating. I stayed in two-star hotels that had more comfortable bathrooms and bedding than a three-star. There is huge variation within each category. One and two star hotels are just fine for tourists who want to spend their money where it really matters.

Key cards have become ubiquitous in the US—the room key that looks like a credit card and is slid into a slot near the handle or held to a plate above the handle—but they are uncommon in Italy. Italy still uses regular old keys, often with a heavy fob attached with the room number etched on it. If you have it in your pocket, you really know it. The idea is that you're supposed to leave it at the front desk when you leave and pick it up when you return, not carry it around with you all day. I found they are nonjudgmental about your comings and goings.

When you are in your room, you're supposed to leave the key in the keyhole in the door, with the fob dangling. The idea is that it blocks anyone who might attempt to peek in through the keyhole. I can't imagine anyone really doing that these days, but who knows.

Italian hotel room keys need two full revolutions of the key to actually lock the door; the first rotation is a primer rotation, so to speak. These doors do not lock behind you; you'll have to do the two full revolutions when you leave the room too. Don't forget and do one rotation!!!! The door is not locked.

If you do get a key card and haven't stayed in a hotel with them before, good news! It's perfectly acceptable to ask for a staffer to accompany you to the room and show you how to use it. The reason is that there are many different kinds and some of them need a certain hand gesture or require split-second timing. Even people who have used them ten times before can find themselves hiking back to the front desk because they couldn't make the thing work. It is appropriate to tip your helper.

Google the words **Hotel star ratings in Italy** to read more about the rating systems. As you can see below, the rating has more to do with the lobby and staff skills.

Teleport the usual Motel 6 to Rome and it could meet the basic criteria for a four-star hotel. That doesn't mean Italian four-star hotels look like Motel 6, they're more like smaller versions of the top floor of the downtown Hyatt, and priced even higher.

One-star hotels. Reception is open at least twelve hours a day; daily cleaning; minimum size of two-person rooms is fourteen square meters; sheets changed once a week or per guest stay, whichever is shorter. Most likely to have a shared bathroom. Rooms with a shared bath may have a sink in the room.

Two-star hotels. Longer reception hours, if over three stories has an elevator (which may not serve every room); sheets changed at least twice a week. Daily cleaning. Private or shared bath.

Three-star hotels. All the one and two-star requirements, plus have a bar service, receptionists who speak at least one foreign language and uniforms for the staff. The reception desk is open at least sixteen hours a day. Rooms have internet services and a private bath.

Four-star hotels. All the three-star requirements plus afternoon turn-down service; sheet and towels changed daily; offers laundry services to clients; has parking for at least 50% of the rooms; every two-person room is fifteen square meters min. and bathroom is four square meters min.

Bathroom in a Three star hotel in Florence; fairly roomy for Italy. Bidet next to toilet, stool under the sink, counterspace is catch-as-catch-can.

Five-star hotels. All the features of a four-star, plus reception is open 24 hours a day with a staff competent in three foreign languages; single rooms are nine square meters min. and two-person rooms are sixteen square meters min. Customers have a choice of pillow, down, synthetic or foam.

Bed and Breakfasts. These have features a hotel does not; evaluate whether they're right for you.

Pros

May get to see a real residence, see how the locals really live and decorate

The breakfast can feature local produce and is home cooked

Can be located off main roads, be less noisy

Can be closer to your desired area

Some have a bathroom for every bedroom

Owner can be helpful, make suggestions and phone calls for you that enhance your trip

May allow use of the elegant living room, patio, sunroom

Leaves you feeling like you've really visited that locale

Is the best choice for getting local flavor, if you plan to leave after breakfast and return between 6-9 PM every day

Cons

The breakfast is often no great shakes; little choice of menu, take it or leave it

Often do not take charge cards; many are cash only (no checks)

May have a set time for breakfast, say 7:30, so no breakfast for you if you get an early start

Wants breakfast to be a ceremony; pouts or is uncooperative if you want to grab food and run

Bed quality is a wild card

May not have air conditioning, or has a loud window AC

The dressers and closets in the room may be ¾ taken up with junk storage by the homeowner; you may have only one drawer and a foot of closet.

Bathroom sharing; if private bath isn't boldly stated online, it's shared

Not cheaper than a hotel

Owner can be nosy, pry into your business

Owner may impose curfew or deadbolt the door after a certain hour

They are really put out if you don't leave after breakfast; things like coming in at 3 AM and sleeping to 11 AM will meet disapproval. And no breakfast.

Suffer a spell of being 'under the weather' so you want to stay in for a day and they'll be annoyed. Ditto with working in your room.

You will be asked every day how long you are staying, when you'll return tonight, etc. It ruins spontaneity.

All this said, I stayed in a B&B near the Vatican in Rome and am glad I did. His house rules and curfews didn't impinge upon my plans. Having no common dining or sitting area, he brought breakfast to my room on a tray with a huge pot of tea, which was perfect for me. The street door to his B&B was unmarked, giving me a minute or two of confusion when I arrived. The lady of the house spoke no English, and it was a third floor walkup. The bathroom was the usual cramped retrofit into an old building, and the bed was harder than I was used to. But on Sunday morning, I sipped my tea while gazing at tiled Roman rooftops out of a floor-to-ceiling window, enjoying the delectable, flowery breeze coming in the open window. And then Saint Peter's

Basilica's deep-bellied bells began to pong. I was in ROME. Magical.

~ ~ ~

Concierge. The hotel concierge is limited to plugging the few local businesses that pay 'commissions' to either the hotel or directly to him, so he's a waste of time for restaurant, entertainment, or good bar suggestions. He might be good for dry cleaner or Profumeria directions, but my experience is he advises you to search for yourself ("There might be one up that way a few blocks. . . "). The position is a money-maker for the hotel, and I hear some can secure a hooker, but I can't vouch for that and think it's creepy to even ask. If you've had success with that, keep it to yourself.

Yelp.com and TripAdvisor.com are better sources for good restaurant advice. These can take a location and rank nearby restaurants for you, with map. Just get some Wi-Fi and start hunting.

If your room's drapes don't seem substantial enough to block out the sun or inquiring eyes after dark, it's because you have shutters. In Europe, shutters are real, working pieces of the house, not décor items. At dusk or before bed, you'll have to open the window, poke your head out, undo whatever latch or turn the knob to free each shutter, and pull them closed. The knobs are sometimes on the bottom and sometimes in the middle; rotate it until the shutter clears.

Late Arrival.
One acquaintance suffered a delay on the flight to her wonderful European tour, landing in London several hours later than planned. When she arrived at the hotel at 8:30

PM they told her they just sold the room fifteen minutes ago because she hadn't requested 'late arrival' and they had no word from her. If she phoned the hotel when she landed over an hour before all would have been fine. Due to full hotels they found her a bed several miles away by midnight . . . and her group left without her the next morning after finding she never checked in. She hadn't called the tour company to let them know she was staying in another hotel.

If your plans change, communicate. Always add the magic words 'late arrival' when booking a hotel, regardless of actual arrival time. Some hotels will feel free to sell the room after a certain time, which could be as early as 7 PM. Another way to absolutely hold it is to pay the first night ahead of time. When it's important, don't depend upon the common sense of strangers, much less hope they have Sherlock Holmes-caliber powers of deduction.

To get a hotel room these days you need a credit card (or debit card) for all but the lowest-end of the market. On the other hand, some bed and breakfasts may take only cash up front. Have your antenna up for the payment methods they accept; never assume they will take credit cards.

When you reserve, they may ask questions like smoking or non-smoking, high or low floor (for those afraid of heights or who wish to use the stairs), and possibly feather or foam pillow (for those allergic to feathers).

Novices always get the hotel thing reversed, feeling like a guest in someone's house instead of the boss who is paying their salaries.

My impression is the more a person travels, the more likely they are to return to the desk to request a different room. The one they were given might smell bad, have poor water pressure, be too noisy, have a tub-shower situation they don't like, the closet door is broken, the TV doesn't work, they don't like the heater or air conditioner . . . could be a lot of things. Infrequent travelers just put up with whatever they're given, even if it ruins the vacation for them. I've gone back for a new room because this one was too far from the elevator, was on the wrong side of the building, or I wanted one nearer to the pool. Don't be shy about doing this; it's no skin off their nose to put you on the other side of the building, and if it makes you happy, hurray! Be polite and don't make a mess of the room before changing your mind. Leave it as pristine as you found it.

The way to request a different room is pleasantly and with a smile and a few rounds of thank yous. One man's ceiling is another man's floor, and for every person asking to be away from the morning sun there's someone asking for an Eastern exposure.

Hotel showers. Hotel shower spray can be a bit more sharp and spear-like than you are accustomed to. It's due to calcium deposit buildup. Most shower heads made in the past twenty years are dozens of little rubber nozzles, each one producing a little jet of water. When the shower is too jetty, it can be improved by rubbing your thumb vigorously over the rubber nozzles, bearing in hard, while the shower is on. This will break up the calcium deposits and make the spray softer and more generous. If one of the nozzles is spraying water off to the side, rubbing it like this can correct it. Why don't the hotel cleaning ladies do this? Because they never turn on the shower so have no idea it's miserable to stand under. I have to 'fix' my shower in about 80% of the hotel rooms I stay in.

Bugs

After reading hundreds of hotel reviews, I tune out what I call the 'bug people'–individuals who see bugs everywhere. Fantastical bugs, finger-sized ones or dozens scurrying when the lights are turned on, or get this, not kidding, so many that the brown bedspread was really an undulating sea of bugs.

I admit it's possible there are cockroaches in hotels. Yawn. The only bugs I've seen (so far) are the ones that fly in via the window or walk in through the door. Maybe very rarely one dead one, which tells me their routine bug spraying is working well.

The last ten hotels I've stayed in had some panicky person writing a review about spotting bed bugs, but frankly I find it hard to believe the sheet-changing staff wouldn't get that taken care of immediately, since they're the ones who ball up the sheet and carry the bundle to the hallway.

Because there are proven cases, here's the following standard advice to check for bedbugs: peel back the bedding and check the seams of the mattress for traces of bedbugs — bloodstains or actual bugs. Another way travelers bring bedbugs home is via infested luggage that was placed on bedspreads or mattresses. When packing or unpacking your bag, put it on a non-upholstered piece of furniture — a dresser or one of those folding luggage stands. Putting clothing into dresser drawers may be another way to get bedbugs. Keep your possessions in your luggage or hang things up in the closet instead. It goes without saying, immediately ask for a different room if you suspect bed bugs.

Most hotel rooms in Italy don't have screens on the windows, and you have to open the window to fetch the shutters closed. You will see bugs. Bugs are good for you. We grew up eating bug parts. Oh yes you did.

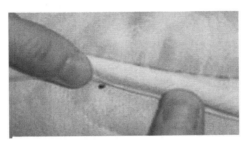

Visual of a bedbug, if you were to go looking for them.

Room Safes

Room safes are a sturdy metal box with a number pad on the front, usually placed in a closet or in the TV stand. Larger ones are sized to fit a computer, but some are smaller. I have never heard of a Break-and-Enter in a hotel by marauding bands of thieves. The unspoken reason for the safe is to prevent pilfering by the staff, who all have keys to your room.

The staff can and will do a few quick knocks on the door and then walk right in if they think you aren't there. If you want to watch TV in the nude with the temp at 75° F, go ahead. Just be sure to fasten the chain latch and/or deadbolt so a barging-in staffer is slowed down a bit. Barging in is not a weird odd occurrence; they come in all the time when you are not there. In the finer hotels they come in around 8 PM to 'turn down the bed' and put a chocolate on your pillow (just like your servants do at home).

Use the room safe for 'attractive' items, not just expensive ones, such as medications, wallets, tickets, jewelry, watches, small electronics and chargers. Even things like the latest hot novel, candy, nail polish and your good pen are worth putting in there when you'll be gone for a couple hours. Leave that half-eaten bag of cashews open on the dresser and when you return if it looks lighter and one has rolled out, it wasn't the wind.

Don't let kids play with the room safe because it has a limit for attempts. If you exceed the allowed tries, usually just three tries, it permanently locks and only the Hotel Manager can open it. Not only is that embarrassing, but he has a day job and might not be back until tomorrow morning.

Single bed and nightstand in a Florence three-star hotel with a rooftop lounge for the free breakfast and evening drinks. A row of switches built into the nightstand controlled the lights here and by the desk. The large window overlooked the street. Because many hotels are repurposed older buildings, rooms have unique layouts. Windows, air vents, closets, lights and outlets may be in odd locations, and there will be bump-outs on walls to accommodate plumbing pipes and electricity to the higher floors. Expect these things when staying in the heart of these old cities.

FLYING TO ITALY

If you have selected a packaged group tour, they will inform you of recommended flight dates. You should get some help from them on airline, airports, best ground transportation, and so on. Just be aware that in their minds your tour starts in-country, so while they help you with selection, all the stuff here about airports, airlines, flying and ground transportation to your hotel is your responsibility. Getting yourself in trouble before you board or getting yourself lost in the Heathrow or Charles De Gaulle airport means you have to figure it out.

First off, use a credit card that includes traveler's assistance. It's in the fine print of the agreement, or can be checked on the credit card's website. When something confusing or tricky happens in the midst of your travel plans, if you bought the airfare with a credit card that offers traveler's assistance as one of the benefits, you have a little help coming from them. Have those domestic and overseas phone numbers in your phone's contacts list plus written on a paper in your wallet in case your phone breaks or is stolen.

They have experience and can give timely advice. They can look things up on a computer monitor for you. They might have someone on staff who speaks the language you need, or can muddle through with a translation program like Google translate. It's free. The stress of travel added to the noise and strangeness of the airport can leave you literally unable to dream up what to do next. They can talk you through it.

Picking the Flight, Getting the Ticket

Where to start, if you aren't taking a group tour?

One, pick the dates and duration based on your vacation days and schedule. Then shoehorn your travel plans into it.

Two, figure out all your must-sees and must-dos from internet searching, then figure out what is first, second, third and so on, then figure out reasonable travel routes and methods between them, throw in some non-earmarked time, then see how many days that is. It's better to develop a max-min time, then hunt the available flights.

Either way, desirable things that break your heart to miss will have to fall off your list. I will console you with the thought that if you had endless time and wealth to do everything, it would all mush together in your memory. Because you are able to do only ten things, they will all be delectable and crisp in memory. You are so lucky to have limited time and money.

The second way is a three-step process. You rough in what cities you want to visit and for how long, rough in how you will travel around, and rough in a month. Then you see what kinds of flights are available. Then you probably change your duration or travel dates a bit, back and forth like that until you're somewhat happy with it.

At this stage, Google the country and the cities you will be staying in, looking for problems. Things like major events that will tie up every hotel room, close down streets or the attractions you want to visit. Are they shooting a movie in the Colosseum? Is it the Pope's birthday? Is that museum open to only groups on Thursday? I can't even begin to predict what it will be. Just look, to the best of your ability. Have a teenager look for you.

Bending your trip around these things before buying the plane ticket is key to your enjoyment. If you're doing this six months ahead, things will come up after you book. But do your best.

~ ~ ~

There are three huge ironies about air travel. First, taking two planes generally is cheaper than just going straight there. Even when you go way out of the way by hundreds of miles. It lands, you disembark, sit around, then get on another plane, with all the extra gas, employee assistance, baggage transferring, and beverage service that entails. They charge a premium for going straight there, while connections are the 'normal' price. If you take two connections (three legs) the price is even lower.

Second, flight prices between the same two cities can vary widely by time of day and day of week, with the airlines charging more for 'desirable' flights. Expenses to them are exactly the same.

Third, is there is no relationship between distance and cost of flight. Don't expect it. It can be cheaper to fly to Frankfurt, Germany than to Des Moines, Iowa. Round trip from Boston to Charlotte NC with a layover in Chicago can be cheaper than flying Chicago to Charlotte round trip, same flight. Do not assume it always costs more to fly to Rome than to Seattle, WA.

Infrequent flyers can made decisions about where to go based an idea that farther away = more money; heck even old hands do it. For years I didn't go to Hawaii because I thought airfare would be expensive—it ended up costing no more than going to DisneyWorld in peak season!

Twenty Tips About Picking a Flight

This year you can fly to one city and return from another. Airlines now sell only one-way trips. Some websites have a multi-city option; use it if it's there. If you don't see it, book one leg at a time, say Chicago to Rome on June 9. After that one is completely booked, do the return leg, say Milan to Chicago on June 19. You can even use different airlines, if that provides the best times and prices.

You can get help from websites like Kayak.com, Expedia.com, Travelocity.com, Bing.com, Orbitz.com, Skyscanner.com, Momondo.com, Vayama.com and others to enter the date you want to go and the date you want to return, and the city. Let these travel sites do the searching for you, but when you find the flights to-and-fro that you like, don't buy from them. Go right to that airline's website to make the booking. AA.com, Delta.com, USAir.com, United.com, Jetblue.com, AirFrance.us, etc.

There are two very important reasons: one, if the flight is delayed or cancelled for reasons other than weather and you bought your ticket from the airline, they comply with what's called Rule 240 to you get on another plane to that destination as soon as possible, even if it means using a competitor's plane. If you can't fly until the next day, they will put you up in a free hotel room overnight for free and give you free transportation to and from this free hotel, did I mention it's all free? If you bought your ticket from 'a third party' which is what the search sites are, you have to contact them for help by phone, they don't have a counter in the airport. Their customers are the ones sleeping in the airport overnight.

Airline customers: sleep in hotel for free.

Travel search website customers: sleep on floor in airport.

Which one is you?

In the event this delay happens, when they are preparing the voucher for the hotel, ask to stay where the pilots stay. It's always the nicest place.

Most airline flights are milk runs. By that I mean the airline will have a 7:10 AM or a 4:35 PM flight from city A to city B every day of the week. If the time doesn't work for you, it's unlikely looking at next week or next month is going to produce a slightly later flight. You'll need to look at another airline or make this time work for you. While the flights are milk runs, the gate may not be the same from day to day. Generally, an airline has a range of gates it has reserved in each airport and the next plane goes to an empty one. They don't give it a lot of deep thought. Gates are decided one to three hours before the plane pulls into that airport.

The later in the day, the higher the odds of a plane being late or delayed. Planes often land for only thirty minutes then are back up in the air, so bad weather anywhere can have a snowball effect across the country four or five hours later.

Don't be overly swayed by gathering up frequent flyer points. These rack up at a penny a mile, and while it's just fine to choose a sole airline for your business travel, your vacation time is too precious to accept less-ideal arrangements for the sake of about $50 in points. Keep the real value in perspective. Losing a half day on either side just to stick with this airline and gain $100 in points, is that a good trade when it's your once-in-a-lifetime trip to Italy?

Speaking of less-than-ideal arrangements, the travel sites can show you airfares a day or two on either side of your trip, which might reveal you can save $100 or $200 by flexing your travel plans. If making this decision merely to save money, please do the math on ALL the costs. Will you have to incur another hotel night and three more restaurant meals? Will parking cost another $22? Every time I've done the math, airfare that's $200 less by shifting one extra day ends up saving pennies.

Conversely, lopping a day or two off this precious trip when you might never come this way again to save an amount like $150 will seem absolutely ludicrous four years from now. If you are gearing the trip to your available vacation days and you opt to spend one of those days padding around the house in stocking feet instead of eating the best gelato in Rome from Cremeria Monteforte while gazing at the Pantheon, come over here I want to smack the side of your head.

Seriously, not all plans can be shifted neatly left or right. There's got to be another way to belt-tighten $200 over the next year; sell underappreciated gifts on Ebay, grow peppers in pots, or my favorite, saving money by eating less, aka dieting.

Spell accurately. When you buy the ticket online, type the name that is on your ID. If you use a nickname or change the spelling even a little, it will mean hassle and possibly not getting on your flight. When buying a ticket for a traveling companion, get the spelling of their name exactly as it is on the ID they will use.

Frequent Flyer points. Overseas travel is not a good use of your points. Not only is it hard to get the best flight times without booking eleven months ahead (and you could go in four months otherwise), but they tack on so many charges that aren't covered by points that you will feel like an idiot for incurring all that delay and fuss for a savings of about $500 a round trip. For the same points you can make two domestic round-trips that normally cost $500 each, with a tiny airport fee. Or you can upgrade about six round trips to first class for the same points. Earn points with overseas trips, use them for domestic flights for the best bang for your buck—um, point.

Picking the flight by connecting city. Frequent travelers do this often. For Italy, you may have a choice of connecting flight within the US, say Newark, Detroit or Boston, and connecting flight outside the US, say in France, Spain or England. Although it can seem exciting to spend an hour in a bonus country, lean in favor of the US layover. Three reasons: one, a two-leg trip with one short and one long leg means less-interrupted sleep; maybe you'll sleep on only the long leg. Two, less stress. If you get lost in Newark you ask questions and understand the answers, but not so in France. Three, if your checked luggage doesn't make it, friends or family back home can take the reins in sorting it out and getting it to you without incurring international calls.

If you have a choice between a one hour gap between flights or a three hour gap, what you chose depends upon your tolerance for risk. Shorter = more risk. On flights to your destination the longer gap is safer, even with carry-on luggage only, because this provides space if the first flight lands late. It is unknown and unknowable what gates the two planes will be parked, close or far away. My experience is they are usually about as far apart as they can be more often than not, meaning twenty minutes minimum from one to the other. If you're seated in row 27 it might take fifteen minutes just to get off the plane. If you're not an old pro at this airport or with flying in general, stick with layovers longer than ninety minutes.

Early morning flights have the best on-time performance, so short layovers are less of a gamble. Odds of luggage not making it to the connecting plane go up after 5 PM. A two-hour layover provides the best odds. A very long layover, say five hours, is also risky, because they have to stash your bag in the corner for half their shift or over a shift change and it could be forgotten.

Same layover city for both trips, or different? Go for best flight times; sticking with the same airport for the second layover because you believe you will be more familiar with it on the second visit won't pan out. A lot will have happened in the past days and what you remember will be a thimbleful. It won't help you navigate, because hub airports are always huge. The corridors you navigate between return legs could be entirely different than the ones you saw going there. The advantage of having been there once before is dinky.

To get a low price regardless of seat, set up a travel 'bot to keep an eye on prices for those to-from airports on a range of dates instead of checking constantly. It will email or even text you. Kayak.com and other sites have the feature.

When to buy? That is a factor of where you wish to sit. The earlier, the more seat choice. How far ahead you can book depends on the airline. Some allow up to a year in advance, others only six months.

Most airlines allow you to view available seats a screen or two before you pay. You can check the seat availability, and decide when to drop the money when there's still a few of your favorite location left, whether window, aisle, near the front, left or right.

Picking the seats. Sitting side by side is an obvious choice. Consider selecting aisle seats in the same row for both people. You're side by side for easy conversation but neither sits in a middle seat.

When both parties wish a window seat and one is a minor, put the minor behind the adult, not the other way around.

Parents instinctively want to keep an eye on a minor child or teenager, but on an airplane a minor is much less anxious if he or she can see the parent at will, knows when the parent gets up or speaks to someone, and can alert the parent instantly without turning his or her head by simply darting out a hand to poke a shoulder, if some issue arises. A parent in front can hear what is said behind them, often more clearly than they can hear the person next to them. If you are given split seating a few rows apart, place the minor more to the rear for the same reasons.

Flight prices drop when there are only middle seats left. If you book late when only middle seats are available, it's still possible to snag an aisle or window seat. Begin checking online for newly-available seats two or three days before the flight, and persist. Phone too, asking what seats are available. If nothing, inquire two to three hours before the flight. If still nothing, inquire at the booth at the gate. Other passengers who buy slightly more legroom seats and exit row seats, which are offered only on day of flight, have their old seats become available. In addition to last-minute cancellations, the first row of coach opens up. Many airlines do not book the first row in coach, saving them to offer to women with babies or toddlers; if your flight has none or only one, the seat can be yours.

Pick a seat assignment when you book the flight, even if you don't care. Each airline website is different, so hunt for that seat availability button, icon or cartoon of a seat. If you missed it, you can always open your reservation using the confirmation number, find the seat map and pick your seats. You aren't stuck; you can change it as much as you like. If you check that plane on Seatguru.com later on and find your seat does not have a window or is a non-reclining seat, still time to change.

Not all airlines allow third-party buyers to pre-pick the seat. This means buyers through the search websites get assigned what is left on the day of the flight, after the airline customers took all the good ones weeks ago. This is another compelling reason to buy only from the airline, never the search engine.

Price changes. On the internet, the price can change if you poke around a site too much or revisit over a few days. How it does it is with cookies, little markers that appear from your computer visiting their site. This is not the same as malware that counts keystrokes; the part of the software that sees the computer at portal XDF433599-4403-3885 popped back three times in forty minutes so changes the pricing profile from D1 to D2 doesn't know or care who you are. This is why doing the searching and thinking at one of the multi-airline search sites and then opening the airline's website to book, when you have credit card in hand, gets you the best price. One visit, like a hawk, swoop and off with your prize.

Some experienced travelers go so far as to conduct their initial searches on their work computer, decide, and then swoop in at home. Some even hike to the local library to do the preliminary searches, then go home to book. I'm not kidding about this, the website keeps track of 'node' and how long it is poking around, and the more you look like a serious buyer, up goes the price. It's not peanuts either, it can be $200 to $500.

On one business trip from Boston to Atlanta, the first time I looked at one airline, all the flights were the same price regardless of time of day; later than afternoon when I went to book, only the before 7 AM and after 8 PM flights were that price; the nice mid-day flights were almost double. I had to leave eight hours earlier than I wanted due to company rules that dictated the booked flight may cost no more than 125% of the cheapest flight that day. For grins, two days later I checked from my home computer, and all flights had returned to the same low price.

Seat map. I prefer the airlines like Delta that provide a 'View Seats' button (the words are the button) right at the deciding point, instead of putting it just before you give the credit card number. Either way, be aware you can go entirely through the process, even up to entering a credit card number, and end the whole thing by clicking the upper right hand X to close the internet window. There are lots of ways to exit the process and only one path to getting a charge on your charge card, so step off whenever you feel like it by just leaving the site.

Prices vary mainly by flight month and how close the flight day is. The example here is for July 10th, searched six weeks before that date, Boston to Rome. This is the round trip price even though the return trip isn't showing here. A Friday flight for May 16, booked in January, was only $1030. Wait until May 8th and that same flight was $2050 with only middle seats left.

FCO is Rome's airport.

Once you have figured out the airline's website, bought ticket(s) and picked seat(s), the airline will send you an email. Print this out, you will need the code written there the day before the trip to print out the boarding passes. Stuff happens, things get deleted. Print it.

Don't thank your lucky stars if you book a seat on a flight only half-full three weeks from takeoff. Airlines cancel routes less than 90% full on the day of the flight. All the stranded passengers have to elbow and bluster themselves onto another flight to that destination over the next two days. It would be better if they cancelled three days ahead, but most of the time passengers get notified three to six hours before. This is when buying directly from the airline's website and not from one of the search websites is worth its weight in gold. Search website buyers have to run around finagling a new flight from scratch and fight to get reimbursed for the cancelled flight weeks later. The ones who booked with the airline have priority for getting another flight.

Premium coach seats. They are coach seats with a few more inches of legroom. They are not business or first class and usually confer no more benefit than a seat assignment and possibly boarding three minutes earlier. Each airline features them differently in the online seat maps. Some show them as available and allow you to select them, but the next day if you revisit the site you're listed has having no seat assignment. That's because you didn't pay for it.

Airline rules change faster than web technology or software can adjust to. The airlines aren't going to discourage choosing a premium seat, but they haven't figured out how make a seat choice lead directly to a credit card payment page. Also, they can't seem to tell you what the extra charge would be upon clicking it.

That's as of this writing; it could have changed last week. Be aware that if you think you're gaming the system, you could have no seat assignment at all.

Sometimes any leftover premium seats might be offered for say, $39 on flight day that are $129 if reserved four months ahead. It's possible there are no premium seats left by flight time, so decide how important it is to you ahead of time.

Picking a seat doesn't mean it's yours. You also have to get your boarding pass early. See *Day Before the Trip* section for boarding pass information. If a plane has a handful of empty seats, it's yours. But most flights are overbooked, and an hour or two before the flight your seat will be handed to a no-seat-assignment guy. If you're in line, you could literally be just behind the guy who usurps your seat. So print out the boarding pass the night before, or arrive three to four hours early to stand in the line, then go eat or explore the airport.

Tip: when returning from Italy, ask the hotel's front desk to print out your boarding pass. I'm going to stick my neck out and say 100% of them will do it, plus 95% of B&Bs. All you need is the airline name, your name, plus your confirmation number—which you write in your calendar plus have on a bit of paper in your wallet.

The couples trick. This may not work well anymore, but I'll share it anyway. On planes with three-across seats, a couple booking early would pick the aisle and window seats in a row, hoping that by flight time no one will be assigned their middle seat. Result: more room, more overhead bin space. If the middle seat does get assigned and the couple really prefers to sit together, they have to sweet-talk the middle person into switching to either the window or aisle seat.

What's a good airline to use? The question is impossible. The true answer, there is no good airline, is of no use. Every airline has its hate club. Each has not ten or twenty but hundreds of people who make it their mission in life to bad-mouth that airline.

Some of the problems are systemic, and it was just luck of the draw that this person encountered it while using that airline, or maybe five or six incidents while using that airline. People in hub cities hate their primary airline the most. If you fly enough, you'll have stories.

The real answer is, you need to take the reins of your flying experience. Keep the trickiness and special needs to a minimum. Study the airline rules and comply. Be your own advocate. Speak up when there's still time to do something about it. Don't count on others to see your predicament. Even when you're upset, take a breath and describe the situation in clear, unambiguous words, do not keep saying "I'm upset! I'm so angry! This is awful!" or use swear words that shed no light on your situation. A happy trip should not depend upon the intuition of strangers.

Airports

The good news is that airports have developed a protocol and procedures that are consistent around the globe. If you know what to expect at one airport, you know them all. The layout is another matter. No two are alike. It's feasible to never study an airport map at all, just follow the signage. But it can be less stressful if you know the lay of the land and have a rough idea whether Gate B and Gate D are five minutes apart or twenty-five minutes apart, or the checked bags will appear for pickup way on the opposite side of the airport, so you can meter your speed accordingly. Airports have maps on the airport's website; usually you have to click through some menus to find it. Sometimes it can be sent to a printer.

One of the magazines in most (but not all) seatbacks will have 'airport maps' on a couple of the last pages. These are so stylized and vague that they end up being little help, but they can shed light on whether you'll need to board an in-airport shuttle train or which direction to head after you land.

Airlines partner with other airlines. For instance, Delta partners with Alitalia, so while you think you've bought a seat on a Delta flight earning Delta frequent flyer miles, at the airport it's the Italian airline both ways. Adapt, don't get stuck on finding Delta; if the flight number is the right one, it is yours.

All airports have:

Almost no clocks in the public areas.

People making mistakes about the time in the layover city and missing their flight.

Parking, long-term and short term.

Short term parking is way more expensive and is charged by the hour, not day.

Slightly more economical parking off-site or farther away that provides a free shuttle bus to bring you to the terminal (airport). It arrives irregularly and no one can tell you how long until the next appears. The driver merely goes back and forth, so distance determines the interval.

Different Arrivals and Departures areas, which are often on different floors. Arrivals are usually below.

A baggage delivering carousel, or several, in the Arrivals area. The term is carousel, although it looks like a tipped conveyor belt.

For Departures, a big open area lined on one or two sides with counters, with each airline having a section of the counter in proportion to the amount of flights it has going in and out.

Lines are formed in snake fashion with waist-high pillars joined by car seatbelt material, and it's considered very improper to go under them, even if it means you weave through empty space to get to the front.

A scanner station manned by TSA employees, to scan carry-on bags and people, located between the airline counters and the 'gates'—gates are gathering areas for a flight. It's a term. Gates are numbered, in sequence—usually.

A requirement that all travelers have a boarding pass to proceed past the scanners.

Well-marked large and frequent signs for gate locations.

Food and drink retailers, mainly major fast food chains, both before and after the scanners; however drink (and mushy foods) purchased before the scanners will need to be discarded in the garbage cans just before the scanners. Count on eating it before going through the scanners.

Food and drink that is purchased after the scanners may be brought onto the plane without issue.

No-fly times when planes cease taking off and landing in the middle of the night. The time they cease depends on local ordinance; some are as early as 10 PM, others 1 AM. If your evening flight is delayed past that time, you cannot fly anywhere until morning.

Flights that begin again, depending upon local ordinance, between 5:30 AM and 7 AM.

Staff who hate when travelers ask them the time.

Lots of people milling about, waiting. Lots of sturdy chairs that actually get worn out from fidgeters.

Airport staff and helpful people who will give you wild-guess directions and advice rather than admit they don't know.

Electronic 'boards' high on walls or hanging from the ceiling that list airline, flight number, gate letter-number, and the time it will arrive (or leave). In general, it can be counted on that the flight will never leave sooner (unless all ticketed passengers are on) but it can leave later. More than two hours before the flight, the gate, flight time and whether it is cancelled or delayed are unreliable. Walk back to one of them to check again one hour before the flight.

Nice restrooms. Sufficient restrooms.

Drinking fountain by the gate restrooms that you can use to fill an empty water bottle.

For Arrivals, signage with arrows using symbols for bus, hotel shuttle, train, taxi locations. Baggage claim signs with arrows.

An area where local (or downtown) hotels provide free shuttles to their building. Often, not always, no evidence of being booked at that hotel is required to get on.

Signs that get you close to the location for bus, train and taxi. It is usually not obvious where these actually are from the position of the last sign. You may need to ask someone who works at the airport after the signage peters out.

All planes have:

Seatbelt extenders, if the belt doesn't quite reach around you.

One to three magazines in the seatback pocket in front of you that you may read and take with you if you like.

A wax paper bag in the seatback pocket that you are supposed to use if you feel like throwing up.

At least two bathrooms.

Skinny aisles.

Louder engine and air noise in the rear of the plane than nearer to the front.

Tray tables that can be used to prop a book, a computer, or set food on.

An emergency exit training class early in the flight that causes new flyers anxiety but bores the rest.

Beverage service with rolling carts and a process for serving drinks so time-consuming and in crying need of an industrial engineer to remove all the non-value-adding motions that it often takes over an hour for a pair of servers to pour thirty cups of juice and twenty-five coffees each.

A flight attendant that opens and closes a drawer 180 times to serve 180 bags of nuts (or shortbread). I keep hoping one of these days she will grab three at a time and reduce that to sixty open and closes.

Drink and food service that starts at the front. They run out of the 'good entree' before the last six rows. On flights less than two hours they may run out of time before they serve the final rows and simply secure the cart for landing.

Flight attendants who keep an eye on the bathroom so a couple doesn't go in together, ostensibly to join the 'mile high club.'

Staff who come around after drink service with a garbage bag but don't make eye contact and walk by swiftly, leaving your little pile on the tray table.

Windows and reclining seats, except in those locations where they don't, and obstructed views by the wings.

Inadequate pressurization; how much ear pain and temporary deafness you have upon landing depends upon whether the airport is at sea level or higher. Picking a higher airport for layovers, like Salt Lake City or Denver, if all else is equal, reduces pain if you are prone to slow ear adjustment when flying, since at ground level SLC is 12.6 psi, not 14.7 psi like at the coasts. Planes pressurize because up where they fly it's about 5 psi, but each psi costs money so airlines vary on how well they do it. If they pressurized to 12 psi you would barely feel anything in your ears on landing.

Credit-card only payments for food and alcoholic drinks on the plane, if they aren't clearly stated to be included when buying the ticket. Saying food is 'available' means it can be purchased.

Not as much drinking on flights as there used to be. If you need fortification for the flight, arrive early and grab a snootful at a bar after the scanners, or get one 'to go' if local ordinances allow that.

Flight attendants who have more emergency and medical training than you think.

Things to Know About Commercial Flying

Armrest. The middle person gets both armrests; the aisle person has the outer one and the window person has the one on the wall. The middle person should try to keep their arms tight and not extend beyond the armrest into the neighboring passenger's space.

In planes having a 3-3 or 3-2 seat configuration, there is sufficient room for one 21-inch high roller bag per passenger; it gets tight only when passengers put two bags each up there. It is permissible to shove widely-space bags as firmly as necessary to fit one more in—but no cursing or comments. Because the space is defined as 'first come, first serve' the flight attendants are forbidden to ask previous loaders to remove—but you are free to ask. The airline staff may not, only passengers may discuss it. Since people may unthinkingly place all their bags and packages up there out of habit with no intention of rudely delaying the plane's departure because your bag must be taken below, bringing the situation to their attention prevents them from bearing the onus of the entire plane considering them rude. If your bag won't fit because it needs three more inches, asking a family to stow a shopping bag or large purse under the seat is reasonable. Pleasant tone of voice is everything.

If a flight attendant spots this going on he or she might give you a hard time, but something you and another traveler work out is fine; just say "I got this, it's a mutual arrangement, there's no problem."

Proper gratefulness to the shopping bag or purse-mover, expressed by giving them your airline mag with the Sudoku puzzles still blank or offering some gum at landing, suffices.

To the airport. Consider wearing your best outfit to the airport. Doing this enhances the odds in any benefit-of-the-doubt situation encountered, whether trying to finagle a first class seat upgrade, having the flight attendant referee a dispute with a fellow passenger, or trying to pass off that you 'forgot' that bottle of liquor was in your carry-on luggage (it's a goner).

Temperature on the plane. Once the plane is in the air, whether summer or winter, it's below zero out there. You're above the treeline, above the snow-covered peaks of mountains. It gets cool on the plane, and down by your feet it could be 55° F. Don't select footwear with the baggage scanners in mind because that's thirty seconds of inconvenience; pick footwear for the long hours on the plane.

That said, planes can be paused on the tarmac waiting their turn on the runway for a long time. In warm weather it can be miserably hot. Airplanes have the inexplicably poor design of having neither air conditioning nor heat when the plane is parked, or not enough to be effective. Dress for cool weather even in summer, but a tank top under your clothes can be handy. If you're in for a hot wait after taxiing out, immediately divest those shoes, get to bare feet and tank top if it was underneath your clothes. Don't maintain dignity until you've sweated off twelve ounces of fluids you're going to need. Some of these waits are horrible, and it's unclear why the flight crew are unwilling to do small things to make it more bearable, but count on that to be the case.

About 70% of airplane travelers are not aware that above their seat is a valve that rotated one way allows cool air to blow on them, and turned the other way will shut it off. There is also a light aimed at your chair.

These two controls are yours to do as you like. Please do turn on the air on whenever you feel a tiny bit warm and turn it off when you don't want a breeze on you anymore. Turn on your personal light when you're going to read or do puzzles, and turn it off when you wish to nap.

Many people will suffer with blowing air or leave the light on while they attempt to nap, not touching them from their initial positions. There's no reason for this. Flight attendants ceased telling travelers about these twenty years ago, figuring everyone knows.

A third button is there, the 'call stewardess' button. Use this button for anything the flight attendant might help you with, but also to inform them if you need to race off the plane to make your connecting flight or need them to arrange a golf cart to rush you to your next flight. While you can't make phone calls, they can. They can even hold the connecting plane for five or ten minutes—but only if you tell them a half hour or more before the connecting flight is scheduled to take off.

Checked bags. In the olden days, people locked up their luggage. After a few explosions on planes due to bombs in the luggage, airport staff were hired to screen every last bag, which included poking around in them at whim. If you locked the lock, they broke it. Special locks for airplane luggage were invented, locks that the baggage handlers can open. Only those are installed on newer bags in stores today.

I'm sorry, but what's the point? The only theft risk is from the baggage handlers, the people who are paid to poke around in your bag, the ones who can open it as easily as their own pants zipper. No one else comes within arm's reach of your bags. Their union fought hard, diligently and relentlessly, and heck they won, to ensure that when the airport baggage handlers inspect your bags, not only are there no cameras or supervisors in the room, but the handlers themselves are not frisked and their lunchboxes or backpacks are not examined when they leave work.

If you think this is a really bad scenario, write your congressman.

So you know when it happens to you, the practice is to take merely one item from a bag. Often the most expensive item will be left behind; it will be the second or maybe the fifth most expensive thing in your luggage. The owner might not even notice it's missing for a day or two. Because higher value items were not taken, traveling companions usually begin blaming each other for leaving it behind or being careless. The theft is never reported.

If you find yourself thinking "Where's my ----?" while unpacking, call to report the theft immediately. Some airlines attach time limitations to reporting missing items, such as within four hours of discovery—day or night. Totally unpacking and inventorying everything may not be what you want to do within several hours of landing, but it's what you must do to be compensated for the loss.

Legal theft, airport style. One item per bag, often not the most expensive. The item can never be recovered because by law they cannot grill the employees to find who took it. Write your congressman if you think that's goofy. Airports are federal jurisdiction.

Until the baggage handlers are legally videotaped every minute, frisked when leaving the area and lunchbags inventoried twice daily, they will keep stealing. Call the airline ASAP to report something missing from your baggage. If your travel companion is certain it was packed, believe them and get compensated for the loss. I had a blouse taken once; don't presume to know what will catch the fancy of a baggage handler.

Incidentals money. If you checked a bag and it's missing when you arrive in Italy, most airlines will either reimburse you for reasonable expenses, up to $50, or give you that amount to get you through the day. Depending upon the case you make with the agent, a larger reimbursement might be granted. If the luggage takes more than twelve hours to find you, some airlines, like Delta, will also reimburse the checked bag fee in the form of a coupon off future flights.

Once you find the baggage service desk, ask the clerk what to check on the baggage claim form or for the relevant form for expense reimbursement so they don't bounce your request later on a technicality. Save your receipts for items like makeup, socks, sun hat, sweater, hair spray, underwear, deodorant or whatever you purchase during the time your luggage is unavailable. These receipts may be required to get reimbursed for your actual out-of-pocket costs.

It's vital to have the hotel name(s) and addresses for the places you'll be staying for the next four days handy, or else the process of getting your luggage back is going to be time-consuming and a pain in the neck. It is also vital to communicate with the hotel staff about the tardy luggage.

I've heard more than one story about the luggage being sent back or being stored in the hotel's luggage room waiting for the owner to claim it.

If your compensation doesn't go smoothly on the first try or your claims are high, most airlines practice stonewalling. People requesting compensation for their out-of-pocket expenses or even totally lost luggage are met with the outrageous demands of 'proof' for every item in the luggage. The Department of Transportation requires airlines to compensate passengers for provable loss up to $3,300 per passenger for domestic flights and $1,742 for international. If the airline is being uncooperative or has disallowed necessary expenses, go to www.dot.gov/airconsumer to fill out an online complaint. If that has no effect, filing in small claims court, which can cost between $25 and $75, often prompts them to settle with you.

Selecting Luggage

Airlines are starting to set weight limits for carry-on bags; for those flights a light bag isn't just nice, it's necessary. The large airlines in continental US have not set limits (yet) but several of the large foreign airlines weigh your carry-on. Depending upon the plane, Alitalia limits each carry-on to 21 pounds (10kg) or 17.6 pounds (8kg), Air France 26 pounds, Virgin Atlantic 13 pounds, Lufthansa, 17.5 pounds. A complete list of the major world airlines is at www.airfarewatchdog.com.

The reason to do carry-on only isn't to save money. It's to save your trip. I plug for carry-on only, but if you have a non-stop flight and if you physically hand over your bag in the sweet spot of two and a half hours to 45 minutes before the flight, then retrieving your bag at your destination is reliable enough to gamble on. Any other scenario and all bets are off.

This may be your once-in-a-lifetime trip to Italy. Business travelers, people visiting relatives or people coming home can check their bags if they like. You don't want that baggage carousel to coast to a stop with you still standing there waiting for your luggage.

Even if you brought enough stuff in your carry-on to tide you through for two days, your next two hours will be finding the proper office, filling out forms and muddling through the reporting process in a foreign country. The stress will be murder. Yes, you'll head off to your hotel with assurances that the bag is headed this way and they'll bring it to your hotel when it arrives, but it's all bad, bad taste in the mouth and the possibility of pure joy for the next two days is shot.

The reason to do carry-on is because you want to be happy.

Quote me whatever statistics you like, but snafus happen to first-timers twenty times more often than to experienced travelers. Frequent flyers have routines, change their modus operandi by airline, airport or time of day based on experience, and murmur reminders to staff at key moments so snafus don't happen to them.

Checking bags on the return trip home is different. If there's nothing in there that you would weep to lose, then check a bag.

Airlines say you are allowed one piece of luggage and one personal item. They don't say 'two pieces of luggage.' How you carry the second piece, that personal item, makes all the difference.

If you have a book-bag-size backpack on your back and are wheeling a rolling luggage, there's a risk some staffer will call it two pieces of luggage. Obtain a big cloth grocery store bag, plop the backpack inside it, carry it in the crook of your elbow, and breeze through.

I've seen people stopped because they had two or three personal items. All of them were smallish too. Combine.

It's tempting to fill the available space, but leave room for your purchases. The easiest way to do that is use a purse or fanny pack for the personal item on the way there, and then buy a big cloth bag in Italy for about €4-8. Hundreds of street booths have them, you hardly have to break stride to buy one.

Duffels. Lands End has a great duffel line; I like the two straps that can be snugged to relieve the stress on the zipper. A duffel is easy to fit all the dimensional measurements – it just mushes into the available space—and while you are walking it never gets gum stuck on the wheel, never tips on uneven terrain, and never breaks your stride going through puddles or up and down steps. Some duffel bags have long enough handles so the resourceful traveler can put one over each shoulder and make a backpack out of it. Yet it will have about 40% more capacity than the largest backpack.

When filling it, balance the weight. It rides much nicer on the cross-shoulder strap if the two ends have heavier weight and the middle is soft, no blow dryers or heels bumping on your hip.

Backpacks. When packing, sequence is everything; for the airport, put shoes, electronics and liquids baggie near the top. You don't want to totally unpack the thing if the

TSA wants to look at the radio or shoes way at the bottom of the bag.

A backpack is luggage only, not for daily use in Italy. I can't express it too strongly: Do not go to ANY tours, ANY museums, ANY church with a backpack on. The backpack-bringers are one of the reasons for the long waits in lines.

Backpacks are forbidden anyplace containing valuables in Italy. It's the same rule ALL OVER. It doesn't change from day to day. Yet every day tourists show up at churches, palaces and museums wearing backpacks seemingly unaware what that lump on their back is called, so are unprepared when confronted. The venues have added storage lockers for these simpletons, who then slowly conduct the process of getting their bag stored, sometimes in a distant spot, then stroll back as if they are not holding up a line with 70 year old Grandmas standing bareheaded in 95° F heat. In the time it takes the staff to handle one backpack person, five to fifteen ordinary people could have been processed and let inside. After several days of variations on this theme, I want to slap their slack-jaw faces to get some brain action going. Ahem, sorry if I offend anyone.

Don't do touristy things in the city while wearing a backpack because you will not have it with you anyway. Figure out a way to store your necessaries in a reasonable, medium-size shoulder bag or a fanny pack. This isn't backwoods survivalist territory.

I saw ladies outside the Vatican crying real tears because they weren't allowed in with their backpacks, and know what? I didn't feel bad for them. Every ticket confirmation carries the warning about non-allowed items.

If the backpack is your sole luggage and it's your last day in town, the hotel or B&B will almost always stash it for you.

Yes, it means you have to loop back. If that won't work for you, ask where the backpack storage area is BEFORE you get in line to clog up the works for everybody. Have a heart.

Wheeled luggage. This is the preferred bag type for both carry-on and checked baggage. Each airline allows different combinations of length, width and height, so check when buying the ticket. Look for a clickable word in the title bar, something about rules, guidelines, luggage, or variations of same. The rule at the time you purchased the ticket is the one that applies to you. Because this luggage usually opens as a clamshell or flip-top, rolled-up clothing can be stood on end as detailed in the *Packing* chapter, allowing instant access to everything with no need to unpack.

Liquids quart bag. This will be outside the toiletry bag for the flight. Once you are in Italy they can be integrated. On the last day you'll have to find all your liquids again and reconstitute your liquids bag for the return trip. Sigh. Don't miss any; it can be a big hassle. Actually, I think they invented this rule not for terrorists, but for all the travelers who don't baggie their liquids and then leak all over the

overhead bins. If they ever discontinue this rule, please continue to baggie every liquid for airplane flights.

String bags. I'm a huge fan of these. They serve as an easy daybag (and are an allowed size in museums) holding a raincoat and purchases. They're the perfect size for stashing dirty laundry. Stuffed with some clothing, they become a pillow. Some of them come with outside pockets perfect as map pockets or storing a water bottle.

Fanny packs, or waist packs, as tacky and unpopular as they are now, offer the best protection against pickpockets. Think hard about ruling out using a waist pack for your purse or daybag when traveling outside of the US just because it isn't sexy. Maybe being sexy to passersby isn't really a good goal. PacSafe makes several ultra-secure travel bags with cables in the straps and wire mesh around the bag, protecting it from bag slashers who slice and then dive in to pick up what falls out. Having a trip unmarred by theft or even an attempted theft is a good goal. Walk around all day with your lock-secured fiber safe around your waist with a two-handed latch mechanism on cable-reinforced nylon and you'll swear there are no pickpockets at all.

Money belts. These come in the standard under-the-belt form as well as shoulder harness or lanyard style. They're all meant to be placed under your clothes against your skin. They are not a good place for your ID, all your cash, and papers you need to present while in public. They are good for larger bills, valuable jewelry/coins, and important stuff you won't need until tomorrow or can get during a trip to the restroom. It goes without saying that hiding valuables but then whipping it out in public defeats the purpose.

When using a money belt in hot weather, put all paper in Ziploc bags to prevent getting damp with sweat.

Purse or daybag. If you're taking a pass on the waist pack idea, this is the bag you carry your passport, money, credit cards, lip gloss, sunscreen, bug spray, maps, tickets, pen, adhesive bandages, ibuprofen, fiber tablets, medicines you will use today, jewelry, face powder, spare glasses, pack of facial tissue, earbuds for audio tours, a few hand sanitizer packets, safety pins, paper clips, floss sticks, tube of Carmex, and items that might be used today. It should be small, so it's quite filled up with the listed items. At most, it will also hold a pair of small binoculars/opera glasses or a string bag or cloth shopping bag for carrying purchases. Another great plan is to buy that shopping bag as a souvenir. Every museum gift shop and souvenir cart has them; in Venice

Ultra-light shopping bags can serve as your return carry-on personal item too. These are in Venice. Every street corner has them in all the major cities.

roomy silk bags were sold all over for under €8. If you end up getting three of them from three different cities, every time you use them for grocery shopping you'll be reminded of the trip. How great is that!

The little Ziploc bags that come with clothes and hold a button are perfect for stashing pills, antacids, and small items that can't mingle or get lost. They offer good protection from humidity too, although often they have a little pinhole.

Use a thin, check-book size zippered bag or Ziploc

to hold the adhesive bandages, ibuprofen, fiber tablets, jewelry, hand sanitizer packets, safety pins, paper clips, floss sticks and Carmex, with a second sleeve or bag for other personal items I may not want mingling with my floss sticks. Ziploc bags are fine, unless you don't want the contents to be visible to passersby.

Know what each piece of luggage weighs before you get to the airport. If you don't have a handheld luggage weigher or a large scale, use your bathroom scale to check the bag weight while still at home. Weigh yourself holding the bag and then just you, and subtract. You could simply prop your bag on it, but these scales lose accuracy at the edges of their range, meaning it will be less accurate in the 0-30 lb. range. Being a pound and a half off will be a hassle in the airport. You'll have to pull out some heavy items and wear them.

The Duomo in Florence, i.e., Santa Maria del Fiore Cathedral. Postcards do it more justice; they are shot from better angles, have perfect lighting, and render colors and contrast more like the eye remembers.

SEVERAL WEEKS BEFORE THE TRIP

Find out if inoculations are needed. Visit www.cdc.gov/travel to look up the countries you will visit. Do this early because some require a series of shots and others take time to be effective. Italy requires no special shots, but you should have the normal US ones.

Check your passport. Many countries will not let you in if your passport expires in six months or less. Don't push the envelope; if you will have less than ten months left on your passport the day you leave the US, renew it now.

Get some arm strength. Italy has fewer porters and more stairs than you imagine. If you're taking trains, cabs and walking, enough said. Even if you're driving, lifting each bag out of the trunk several times is unavoidable. It can be as simple as two one-gallon milk jugs filled with water and heaved around while watching TV. Do it like the pros: exercise to fatigue every second or third day, not every day, to build muscle.

Lose weight. An upcoming vacation is better than a New Year resolution for providing the motivation to fit comfortably into clothes. Think of all the photo ops.

Start a packing list. Each trip is a little different. Start with the list here, then modify it. Make notes for additional or unusual things you wish to bring as they occur to you, like "Pack a US flag to wave during the event" because when you're actually packing, no standard list here or anywhere is going to remind you 'US flag.' Ditto if you want to bring balloons to decorate the room for someone's mid-trip birthday or bring specific jewelry. The Notes feature in most smart phones is can be a good place for storing these until you can add them to the master list. Emailing yourself works too. Don't count on spontaneously remembering it later. Have you ever wanted to pick up three things at the drugstore but when you arrived could remember only two? As obvious as it seems at the moment, don't make extra work for your future self. Write down additions to the travel list the moment they occur to you.

Get used to standing. If you have a mostly-sitting job, put more standing into your day. Get your feet toughened until standing four hours per day is comfortable.

Visit the dollar store. All your travel-size product and empty container needs just may be fulfilled for under $10.

Test the ear plugs. Nothing is more dismaying than planning a good in-flight sleep only to find the ear plugs you purchased cause pain or distract you after only an hour or two. Or fall out. On a day when you don't need an alarm clock, try a night with the earplugs. Earplugs can be wiped off with hand sanitizer and a facial tissue or a pre-packaged wipe. Don't use soap and water on the foam kind; the soap can soak into the earplug material and cause skin irritation.

Test run the changes. Stick with your usual deodorant, shaving cream, lotions, hair spray. If you're switching to a brand with a travel size, buy it a few weeks ahead and use it for five days. If you still like it, fine. But if not, you have time to try something else.

Create a gift list. You may think you'll just pick up a few things for family, friends, and helpers, but when you get home with three scarves and four refrigerator magnets that don't seem appropriate for anyone, you're sunk. Really think through the plan that you're going to Italy and are NOT bringing back something for the people taking care of things while you're gone. You can get super-duper mileage from a $14 leather gift from Italy. Having a list and earmarking each purchase for a specific person prevents returning with a small pile of 'gifts' that aren't used. Realizing after you've left Rome that the lady watching your cat would have cherished anything from the Vatican ten times more than a leather wallet from Florence is a missed opportunity.

Arrange pet care for dogs or cats. If considering a kennel, it is less distressing for your pet if you take it for a visit to the kennel ahead of time. On the first visit leave the pet for about an hour, then take it home. Make the second visit four to eight hours, perhaps overnight. A third visit ensures your pet understands that this place is temporary and you're coming back. Too many times people take their beloved pet to a kennel and return a week later to find their grief-stricken pet is never the same again. Never quite as happy or trusting.

Most cats can manage with a daily visit by a neighbor, but you are a better judge of whether your cat is like 'most' cats. Dogs require exercise and at least two longer visits per day. When the dog or cat will stay in the home with only daily caregiver visits, leave a radio on, tuned to a close station with no static or hums, to kill the overwhelming silence. Don't make it loud; low enough to not interfere with conversation is fine because they have pretty good ears.

Cage animals like lizards, rodents, birds, fish and the like aren't so broken up about a change in care; carrying them to stay with someone is better than piling up the food and water and leaving them alone. The time of highest stress and risk is while taking them to the temporary home. Some vacation-related deaths I know about began with the stress or temperature change during the trip to or from the caretakers. Mind the temperature.

Here's one last insight, take it or leave it: avoid having an under-16 person as the sole caregiver for a pet of any kind. A neighbor or friend's child may be willing and may be familiar with its care so it seems OK. This scenario has the highest rate of death or serious complications. You will never get a straight answer on what went awry—even if that honesty is mandatory for the vet to save the animal's life. Speculating, which is all I can offer, my impression is it's one or more of the following: The child misses days. Someone 'hugs' too long. They feed it a 'special treat' human food. They take it outside because all creatures like being outside. They bring friends to see it who do something non-allowed. It bites or scratches them so they punish it. It gets away and they injure it during recapture. They feed it but don't change the water.

If you give a child six things to do and remove supervision, perhaps four will get done. That's because they are children, which is why the law does not let them sign contracts or drive cars—being physically small has nothing to do with it. Their judgment and bearings in the world are not fully formed.

Their intention was to present a happy pet on your return. The reason it didn't happen is because they did not see the poor result coming. A child could believe hugging is nice—with no exceptions for being a mouse or avoiding covering the nose. These fine points are not yet formed. At minimum, get the child's parent to agree to supervise the care. Whatever the outcome, you accept the risk with eyes open. Accept the consequence gracefully. Pay the child the agreed-upon amount even if the pet is dead or harmed.

Buy tickets for your must-do attractions. The silly way to travel: get some travel books, crack them open on the flight over, and decide what to do each morning. In Italy this means a lot of standing in line, often several hours per attraction. Some things like the Vatican and the David statue can't be done at all. If there is something you really want to see, visit that website ahead of time and book the tickets. Buy the tourist card for that city to reduce the line waiting (see the chapter on Tourist cards). Even a tourist card, however, can't get you into sold-out venues.

Get a tan. There's nothing more risky than going nearer to the equator without a tan. Most people going to Italy have a nice indoor job and suddenly change to spending a lot of time outdoors. Sunscreen is sticky and messy and you can only bring 3.4 oz. of it per container, plus in the rush and hustle you'll forget to put it on. A handful of sessions in a tanning booth or just tanning in the yard can increase your tolerance from thirty minutes to burn to three hours to burn. Combined with a hat or baseball cap, and sticking to areas under awnings, this is enough to skip packing sunscreen entirely. If you're worried about health, one tan isn't going to risk your life or make you wrinkle up permanently. We were designed for being in the sun.

Practice climbing steps. Aim for being able to climb and descend 300 steps within about forty-five minutes. The goal is not to do it in one unending stretch; the goal is to do them and *not be sore* the next day. Most tours involve a lot of up and down. Doing this means that if the inclination or opportunity arises to climb to the top of a tower or church, or the elevator is so slow you're willing to take the stairs, you know you can do it without sacrificing tomorrow's busy schedule.

Program your phone's weather button. Usually one comes with the phone, and several cities can be programmed. Get a feel for the weather in the days before leaving. It informs your packing choices. Tip: after a lot of rain comes sunny days, and after a dry spell comes rain. Five days of rain before your trip actually improves the odds of sunny days for you. If you see eight days of sun just before your trip, pack a raincoat.

Pick two or three credit cards. It's safer if one is MC, one VISA, and one whatever you want. Keep all the rest at home. Hunt down the four-digit pins for cash advances, and if you can't find them, apply for new pins. The cash advance can cost only a few bucks more per $200, and if you pay it in full upon returning home (regardless of the payment date), interest charges will be less than the price of a coffee. Even though my bank promised my ATM card would work in Italy, it didn't. I flipped to cash advances. Having the pins could save your vacation.

Hold the mail. This can be done about four weeks ahead, and takes a few days to process. Simply visit www.usps.com and click "Manage Your Mail" then look for "Hold Mail" in the pull-down menu. Fill out the form and you're done. They improve their website regularly so it could look different. Another option is to have a neighbor pick up your mail and newspaper regularly.

Driving. If you plan to drive overseas, you may need an international driver's permit in addition to your regular driver's license; check the individual regulations for your destination country. Most people can obtain this permit for under $20 from an AAA office, the National Auto Club or by mail. Google **International Driving Permit** for more information. You'll need your passport, current driver's license and some proof of your flight. Ideally, apply two to four months in advance.

Suspend newspaper delivery. Like holding the mail, it takes several days to kick in, so three days' notice may not be enough.

THE WEEK BEFORE THE TRIP

Cull through wallet contents. Remove every card that won't be used, library card, business card, etc. Don't lug around a single thing that has no chance of being used. Take your insurance cards along, though. You might even get away with not bringing a wallet at all, if you're bringing a fanny pack or other item that will always go with you.

Pick the carry-around bag. Most travelers decide on something bigger than usual. See the *Selecting Luggage* chapter for more information, and *Packing List* for what should or can go into it. Museums and churches do not allow backpacks, knapsacks, or briefcase-size purses, so tone it back. Your back and shoulders will thank you too. Even if the venue has storage for backpacks, 1) since you have to stow it, you have less stuff with you than people with normal size purses, so why bring it; 2) it takes ten times longer to process you than to process a considerate, less encumbered person.

Inform the credit card companies. Now that you have a few cards with known cash advance pins, go online or phone the issuer to complete a travel notification. Use an end date at least three days past the real end date. This reduces hassle if some businesses are slow in turning in the charges, there's a plane delay, or if you agree to be bumped from the return flight in exchange for airline freebies.

Wear the shoes. Wear your primary pair of shoes for nine hours. Take a sixty minute walk in them. Now's the time to change your mind about which shoes go along. Each trip you take, it's worth having a twenty second talk with yourself on whether buying shoes at the destination works for you. If shopping will be part of this trip, it might kill two birds with one stone.

Tip: if you think a pair of shoes might be rough on the back of your heels or on one of the toes, put foam tape or an adhesive bandage in that spot right from the start. Don't wait until the first layer of skin is gone.

Use the copier. Make two color copies of the photo page of your passport; leave one with someone at home that you can reach by phone, and put one in the carry-on bag (not the same bag as the passport!). Additionally, place all the credit cards, ATM card, Driver's License, international driver's license if you obtained one, and medical cards that you are bringing along on the copier and run two copies. Put one at home where you can easily direct someone to retrieve it, and the other in the carry-on bag. After making the copies, write the 800 number for each card adjacent to it, but never the three-digit code from the back. If you get robbed or lose your purse or wallet, this will mitigate the damage and may even allow you to complete the vacation more or less as planned.

Time

On all trips involving sight-seeing and visiting attractions, time is of the essence. It is too important to leave the responsibility to just one device. Especially if that device is a phone, which can get broken or stolen. Smart phone alarms fail to perform for so many reasons. The wake-up tone or song, which can sound loud at home, may not cut it in a hotel room with a loud air conditioner. Lost opportunities due to oversleeping are a major cause of traveler regrets. A phone is not enough! People forget they flipped the sound off last night in the restaurant or theater and go to bed.

Even if the sound is on, a rendition of "Here Comes The Sun" might not do the trick. Hotel rooms are full of unusual noises that your brain is tuning out for you; what's one more?

Depending upon hotel wake-up calls is foolish. It's fine as a backup. Based on friends who persist in using this method, the odds of getting a call is about 80%. Russian roulette has better odds. Of the calls that are actually made, the too-early ones mean you continue to lay 'for just a minute' and the next thing you know 45 minutes have passed. If the call is fifteen minutes late, that's too much. Worst of all, if the wake-up call never comes, they'll just say you didn't request one. The truth is, people like the wake-up call until it fails. Then they stop. Just stop now and skip that miserable day. Russian roulette.

What about the hotel clock-radio? They're often confusing and partially broken in unpredictable ways. Test it by setting it for ten minutes from now to see if the sound is adequate and not awful. If it passes the test, then set it for tomorrow morning. For me, about 40% of the time it doesn't pass, I can't make it go off or the sound is unacceptable.

The insurmountable problem with hotel clock-radios is that a hefty building with five walls between it and the radio signal is the worst location for a cheap, poor-reception radio. The very essence of qualifying to be a hotel clock-radio is being cheap. The radio station that is strong at 8 PM may be mild static at 6 AM the next morning.

The other requirement is a tiny alarm noise that is inaudible one wall thickness away, or else everyone would be waking the guy next door. This noise often doesn't stand out above the air conditioner fan. So it doesn't wake you up. **A good primary wake-up tool is a digital kitchen timer.** It's small, light, and impossible to confound. Set it for seven and a half hours, press the button, place it out of reach on the nightstand or desk, and it will go off no matter what. When traveling several time zones from home, my track record is that 50% of the time the kitchen timer wakes me up, not the phone alarm I set to go off five minutes earlier, and not the hotel clock radio, ditto. I'm a techy person, so I refuse to take the hit that I'm too dumb to set an alarm clock. It's not my fault; that's my story and I'm sticking to it. The phone is the backup, as is the hotel's alarm clock. Wake-up call, fourth backup. Always engage every possible way to wake yourself up.

Get $1, €1 and €2. Whether traveling in the US or International, hit the ground with a supply of small bills or coins. Tipping shuttle drivers, hotel bellhops, and waitresses is expected and if the smallest you have is a $5 or €5, of course they'll say they have no change. One way to get change is to ask co-workers and neighbors for leftover Euros from a past trip. AAA and banks may be able to provide Euros at a high cost. Count on getting most of your Euros from an ATM at the train station or in the city; then buy a pack of gum or something and ask for coins for change.

Pay Bills. Pay something toward any bill that comes due in the next few weeks. Online you can schedule payments weeks ahead. Even if the due date is a few days after your return, between going through mail, unpacking and other tasks it could be forgotten.

Save phone numbers. Put the phone numbers of hotels, tour guide company, bus companies, train ticket office, airline, and even museums and sites being visited into your contacts list. I make a contact called 'Italy' and list them all in the notes. Also write several of them in tiny print on the back of a business card or type them close together in a Word doc, then shrink it and print, for your wallet.

Keeping your phone on airplane mode the whole trip? Not a problem; everyone has a phone. Just ask a friendly local to call the number for you and explain your predicament. If you're delayed or have issues, you can call the hotel or tour to tell them you're on your way, hold your place. Check and double-check each number, you don't want the number to have the five and six transposed.

Mark your bag. There are so many black bags and similar-looking duffels and backpacks. Customize yours with stickers, ribbons tied on or sewn-on patches on at least two sides to make it identifiable at a glance. Be creative. Even if you don't check the bag, there's hotel storage, shuttle bus racks, overhead compartments and plenty of other chances for mixups.

Get nails done. But only if you are a person who does that. Starting a vacation with fingers and toes at their best instead of sporting three-week-old nail polish just feels better.

Computer. If bringing a computer, do a full backup. Don't forget to backup fonts, favorites, wallpaper and small programs you've downloaded into your Programs folder.

Optional. Spray the outside of cloth luggage, duffels and backpacks with waterproofing spray. This will help keep your belongings dry if you get caught in a downpour.

Garbage. The day before, go through the refrigerator and throw out or give away any items that will go bad before you return. If your cans aren't always out, like in an alley, or your don't have access to a dumpster, find a neighbor who will take your garbage and add it to theirs so it isn't fermenting in the house, garage or elsewhere while you are gone.

For Women only. Pack your tampons or pads, even if your calculations indicate the trip lands between. The reality of female biology is that period timing pulls into synchronicity when living with other women, and sleeping in hotel beds fools mother nature. If you've been in menopause less than two years, pack some when going on a trip, because this may be your last time. Unless you're a very alpha female or sleeping where only men have gone before, hotels will alter your period timing.

Check basement, sheds, windows, etc. Do a walk-around before leaving even if you think all is fine. Once I found a hose that had been shut off at the sprayer, not the faucet, and that spray unit was already leaking badly. From a window cracked open 1" to dirty dishes with food (attracting vermin), a slow twenty minute check of all the places you haven't touched for months could save you much misery later on.

Business sign, Pompeii.
What, me plan ahead? I'll just eyeball it.

DAY BEFORE THE TRIP

Packing the Bag

It's not hard to pack a bag for the least airport hassle; see the TSA chapter for more information. In general, put anything that looks like a bottle or liquids container into the liquids bag. Even if it's only talcum powder, it's better to eliminate all chance of being stopped to take a closer look. If it's larger than 3.4 oz., put it straight into a bin. Biscuit tins, plastic containers, empty bottles of any sort are good candidates for just placing next to the shoes in the bin, so keep them easily accessible in the carry-on.

Put all your electronics gear in one suitcase pocket or one baggie, gallon-size if you need to. All things with cords, little motors, batteries and power supplies can prompt a closer look depending how they lay.

More small things . . .

Turn off the water supply to the clothes washing machine. The washing machine hoses are the location most likely to suffer a burst line.

Scour the house for dirty dishes and leftover food. You don't want to come home to find a colony of bugs or rodents have settled in.

Put a capful of bleach in each toilet after the last use. It prevents anything from growing around the edge.

Record TV shows. Your cable service usually has a website where you can look up the scheduled programming for the next week or two, enabling you to adjust the weekly recordings to catch specials you don't want to miss, or record longer if your favorite show might be delayed due to a game. If you miss a network show that you wanted to see, visit that network's dot-com site, CBS, USA, A&E, NBC, ABC for example, to see if the full show is available for watching on the computer. Often, about four days after airing, it's available.

Printing the Boarding Pass

The ticket for the flight isn't the real ticket. Consider it a loosey-goosey reservation. The real ticket is called a boarding pass. A person can print out the boarding pass from any computer having access to a printer about twenty-three hours before the flight, or arrive early at the airport and get it when dropping off checked bags. These are not equal; the first is time efficient and safe, the second is risky and time-consuming.

To print a boarding pass, visit the airline's website again to look for something like this CHECK IN button. Next to it, as an aside, there's a button to check on incoming flights; if you know the airline, you can check whether the flight was weather-delayed along the way, saving you from driving to pick up guests hours before the plane lands.

Click the check in button, enter the information it requests, which will include the code, and send to the printer.

If you're phone-savvy, you can get the boarding pass sent to your phone and they can actually scan the bar code on the phone at boarding.

If you are doing carry-on baggage only and printed out the boarding pass four to twenty-three hours before the flight, you can head right for the TSA baggage scanner check-through line and not have to stand in any other lines.

Thermostat and electronics. The day you leave, set the thermostat to save a little money on heating/cooling. Unplug appliances that draw power. I like to unplug the TV and all computers just in case there's a power surge while I'm gone. Turn off the water at the knobs to the washer and dryer too, since those hoses are the ones most likely to develop leaks.

DAY OF THE TRIP

Winter flights to warmer climates. The biggest enemy of packing light on trips to warmer places is the winter-appropriate outfit we wear from house to airport and back.

Leave the winter coat, gloves and boots (if you think you'll need them when you return) in the trunk of the car. From car to terminal, wear only a warm hat and a fleece scarf.

No matter how cold it is outside there's no chance of frostbite or dropping dead from cold while walking briskly in the parking lot to your car, or back again. Even if you're in the remote parking, the shuttle bus is heated.

Hat and fleece scarf go in your bag for the trip. On the plane, the scarf makes a good shawl or balled up, a good pillow. I use the fleece for extra insulation for the arm against the window, which gets really cold.

When the climates are about on par, but cold, there will be jackets, fleece scarves, sweaters and the like. If you're this type of person, consider a leather jacket cut something like a blazer or is attractively stylish; it can look sharp and will work both indoors and out, even though it will be heavy. You could probably get away with no sweater at all.

The headband-style ear warmers can be very warm and ball up very small. With the right color, both men and women can pull it down around their neck where it looks something like a turtleneck to the casual eye. These can be very compatible with women's hairstyles, not creating helmet-hair.

Rainwear. Any cloth top, hoodie or jacket can be made into passable rainwear with the liberal application of spray water repellant. We're not talking forever here, just two weeks tops. If you have a jacket you want to wear, don't be so hasty in bringing a second raincoat, consider making this one more water repellant. As they say, test the spray in an inconspicuous place, let it fully dry, to see if it changes anything in a way you don't like.

Car in long-term parking. Clear out personal items visible through the windows before leaving home. Remember to lock the car doors as you walk away. People who suffer break-ins usually had items like jackets, CDs, and other attractive items laying on the car seats. Shoving a bunch of stuff into the passenger side footwell can lead a passerby to assume something nice is being hidden. You may suffer the indignity of having your window broken and then he doesn't even take your hoodies, scrapers, magazines and E-Z Pass toll unit.

Support socks. Sitting too long in a fixed position causes blood to pool in the lower legs. Wearing support hose on all flights, especially the return trip, can reduce the odds.

On long flights for people over forty, circulation problems can happen for the first time. Never think it won't happen to you simply because there have been no warning signs. Stewardesses may insist it doesn't happen, but their flight experience is the opposite of yours. They and all their co-workers are walking around for half the trip. Any passenger who feels something is amiss with a leg as they disembark just adopts a scrunched look and wordlessly exits the plane. No one phones the stewardess to report they're in the hospital two days later.

There seems to be a force at play which blocks the collection of actual statistical data on illness and blood clots related to air flight. Don't hold your breath waiting for the airlines to support this research. Anecdotes are all there are, and anecdotes indicate a significant occurrence rate.

Fortunately the fix is easy. Take ibuprofen and wear support hose to bring your odds of getting blood clots back to where you thought they were in the first place. A little aisle walking and high-stepping one leg at a time in the restroom for ninety seconds is a big help too.

What's the most miserable feeling while on a trip? That moment when you realize something you intended to bring is not there. Often it's literally the one thing you mentally said "Bring the ---, bring the ---" while preparing. Why is it not there? Because you handled it uniquely. You had it in your hand when you left the room to answer the phone or get the laundry. You placed it right in the middle of the dresser so it could be packed last.

It is the same Murphy's Law that causes your favorite DVD to get a scratch (but none of the others), or your favorite t-shirt to be stained before the fifth wearing (no stains on the others). The Boarding passes are still on the dresser, under the sweater you decided at the last minute not to bring. The shoes you must wear to an event are still beside the bed, half under the dust ruffle, because with absolute certainty you recall you packed them first— forgetting that later you changed your mind about which suitcase to bring, removed them and then were engaged in a phone call as you loaded the new suitcase.

Thinking, "I'll never forget those so I'll get them later" or "It's in the carry-on already" or "My traveling companion always brings that" leads to the very thing you wish to avoid: a burst of stress while dealing with a situation that cannot be undone.

This need NEVER happen to you! Or happen again, if it already has. Follow this rule and you will be inoculated against having that miserable feeling.

Eliminate that miserable feeling on a trip by keeping a list and checking it in a very specific manner before leaving the house. Simple, yet revolutionary.

The list should contain all the things you want to bring, even boarding pass, even gum, *even* paper clip, in the days or weeks prior to the trip. No item is too minor if you want it.

Just before closing each piece of luggage and leaving, go through the list by *laying eyes plus touching each item with your fingers* before moving to the next. This is more vital when two people are packing together.

If you pack in dribs and drabs over a few days, block out time before the last close-the-bag to somewhat unpack and do the list from top to bottom. If your list has 'pocket raincoat', do not just look through foggy plastic at it, unzip the container and turn it a bit with a finger. What looks like the raincoat from this angle may be a balled up string bag. Simply looking at the list, mumbling, 'yes got that, and that, and that' does NOT work.

Your list should be grouped by container: Carry-on, checked bag, liquids bag, toiletries bag, nightstand bag, electronics, purse.

To make it easier on myself, I print out a tentative list to carry in my purse, adding items as they occur to me. Later on I type up the list, to keep it for the next time I travel.

Over time I have a couple lists on the computer: Business trip, overseas, family vacation, hotel convention.

There is a perfectly sound explanation why just mentally going through the list doesn't work. Travel is off the beaten path for us so our usual autopilot patterns don't serve us well. We're making decisions on top of decisions and sometimes one reasonable choice messes up an earlier choice. So we find we brought four lipsticks and no hairbrush. Like I did at least three times.

Are there things packed that are not on the list? Sure. Who cares, not me. Anything that will make my heart momentarily sink if I go for it and it's not there is on the list.

Before my last trip I bought a sun hat to bring along; up until now I wasn't a big hat wearer. I packed it three days before leaving, then later hung it on the floor mirror knob to pack last to reduce crushing. I would have forgotten it without the touch rule, because I recalled laying it in. Eyeballs and touch; the only fail-safe system. No item gets breezed by out of certainty.

Using pockets for important stuff is a rich source for snafus. The very-very important item is put into the jacket pocket, but an hour or two later it makes sense to wear a different jacket for some very good reason. Item remains in the closet at home. Or the item is in the front pants pocket and walks itself out during the drive to the airport, dropping to the carpet unnoticed. Or the sweater or jacket is tossed on the car seat or carried over an arm on the way to the airport so the item falls out. Or once at the airport you spontaneously decide to toss the too-warm jacket into a checked bag. Now that you know, this will never happen to you, right?

Print out your boarding pass from a computer and printer 12-23 hours before the flight whenever possible. The line for your airline's boarding passes and checked bags can be long and move very slowly. If you wait until an hour before the flight, your well-chosen seat is nearly always gone.

Wouldn't that be a kicker. You bought your seats five months ago just so you could get seats 7A and C, and now, after two hours of standing in line, your seats are gone so you and the spouse are in seats 27B and 24B. Probably the people who used to have 27B and 24B are now in your seats.

Airlines hold your chosen seat, within reason. If an hour before the flight they have not heard from you, they will give that seat to another passenger with an undesirable seat. People on stand-by are seated fifteen minutes before take-off in the seats of ticket-holders who didn't show. Should they 'know' that if anything happened to you, your relatives would call to cancel? If something so bad happened that you yourself couldn't pick up a phone, giving the airline a courtesy call won't loom large in your loved ones' priorities.

When you print out the boarding pass, indicate whether you are checking a bag. Some airlines have kiosks, little side stands, to weigh and tag checked bags reported this way. You can check luggage without the long line. Be sure you go to the one for your airline. Things are often pretty close together and not clearly marked.

It hardly bears mentioning, but I will, that it's important to really listen to the airport staff when they ask questions and not give agreeable answers in small talk tones. If he chirps "Flying US Air today?" as he tags your bag at the kiosk or she says "Going to New York today?" as she prints the boarding pass . . . when today you are flying to Rome on

United with a three-hour layover in New York, well, this is the way disasters happen.

Correct them! Even if you said uh-huh as soon as you heard the 'U' sound, STOP. Say excuse me, I'm flying on United. Say excuse me, I'm going to Rome, not New York. Take these points of contact seriously.

If you are checking luggage, do it immediately upon arriving at the airport because how long it takes is a wild card. That short line may tempt you to grab a coffee first, but ten minutes later it could be 65 people long. Then head for the scanners, because that's a wild card too.

After you get through, search for the Arrivals and Departures list. These are commonly black electronic screens mounted high on walls or hung from the ceiling, with columns and rows of airlines, flights, destinations and times listed. Walk and look around a bit to spot one. Look for your flight number and airline. Check whether the gate and time match the ones on your boarding pass. If not, go to the ones on the sign. You don't need to get a new boarding pass, but you do need to show up at the right gate.

Travelers older than 75 are allowed to leave their shoes on and may wear a light jacket through security checkpoints. If anything questionable appears during people-scanning, those over 75 can take another pass through the scanner rather than be led off to another room for pat-downs or whatever. If you look younger you may need to ask for your special rights.

Gate assignments can change an hour or two before the flight. When you arrive early or have a long layover, if your flight isn't indicated at the gate counter an hour prior to departure, find a Departures sign for your airline to see if the gate changed. No one will bother to find you and no one will tell you the plane is at a different gate unless you ask.

The cardinal rule of airports is everybody—everybody—keeps their own boarding pass on them at all times. Even very young people. If one person holds all the boarding passes and another member of the party visits the restroom and is checked by a guard en route, being on this side of the baggage scanners without one could lead to eviction. Huge hassle and pain in the neck.

Standing in line. If you are in danger of missing your plane because you're standing in line, are in the rear of the plane with a tight connection, or any similar predicament, bring your plight to the attention of the airline staff while there's sufficient time to help you. Do not sit there and stew. This isn't taking skips. This whole situation is for the purpose of flying customers to their destination, you're a customer, and this is what it takes.

It is way more trouble for everyone if you miss the flight.
Ask for help before the situation is impossible.

IT IS NOT TAKING SKIPS.

It is doing what it takes to get you on your flight. They will call a golf cart to whisk you to your next plane. They will even hold the plane for you. But folks, give them some time to work with, don't hog those last minutes so they have to jump hoops and sprint on your behalf.

It is LESS RUDE to draw attention to your situation with thirty minutes to go, when you can walk yourself to your gate and the plane leaves on time.

Pretend I'm a fellow passenger twelve people ahead of you in line. Me: "Please, you go first, I don't want you to miss your plane, mine takes off in two hours. I'm here early to read my Kindle and sip a coffee." All the other eleven people chime in "Yes, I totally agree, I'm not such a meany that I want you to miss your flight, I'm a nice person."

This is not the grade school lunch line, and the issue isn't the chocolate chip vs. the oatmeal raisin cookie; this is hundreds of dollars at stake and your once-in-a-lifetime venture, and if you don't engage a staffer for thirty seconds of help now, in a half hour a staffer will spend twenty minutes on you, getting you on some other flight.

IT IS NOT TAKING SKIPS.

Short layovers. If your seat isn't near the front of the plane and you have a less-than-45 minute layover, or delays on this flight ate up your layover time, talk to the flight attendant at least half an hour before landing. She can get on the PA to ask everyone to remain seated for five seconds longer to let the passenger in 31C get to the front to make a tight connection. She can have a golf cart waiting for you. Doing this is preferable to requiring the airline to bribe someone to give up their seat on the next flight so you can board that one.

She can check your connecting flight. She may find your connecting flight is also delayed two hours, so there you go. No need to get your stomach in a knot.

You are not a little leaf buffeted by winds, powerless to control your destiny. You are a customer, and every employee will mobilize on your behalf to make sure you fly from A to B with the least hassle to themselves. Flying in the seat you reserved, not taking someone else's seat later on, is the least hassle.

Do not be the last to board. If you hate to stand in lines so think you'll sit in the café until five minutes before departure and waltz onto the plane, think again. If the plane is overbooked they will have given your seat away three minutes ago, even if you have a boarding pass. They'll think, maybe he lost track of time and isn't coming.

Two, when all the waiting people are processed, a gate staffer glances up to see if anyone is rushing their way, and if none, gives the OK to remove the boarding ramp from the plane. About 20% of the time a plane will close the doors a few minutes before the listed departure time. About 10% of the time they're actually taxing away a few feet at the listed departure time.

When a plane is overbooked, a flight attendant will walk up and down the aisles looking for empty seats. Those seats are given away before departure. This is exactly the reason why customers aren't allowed to use the airplane restrooms prior to take-off and everyone must sit down with seatbelt on.

Checked luggage at connections. If there is less than one hour between planes, your bags are unlikely to make it from the first to the second plane. The airline will send them on the next flight to that city. At baggage claim you fill out a form that tells them where to deliver the bags when they arrive. Frequent travelers become indifferent to this. They even like it; now they don't have to struggle their own bag on trains and busses, it just shows up at the hotel ten hours later. Frequent travelers take a photo of their checked bag at home, then print it out so they can attach the printout to the form for easy ID when it arrives.

If you checked a bag and for any reason it's missing when you arrive at your destination, most airlines will either reimburse you for reasonable expenses, up to $50, or give you that amount to get you through the day. Depending upon the case you make with the agent, a larger reimbursement might be granted. If the luggage takes more than twelve hours to find you, some airlines, like Delta, will also reimburse the checked bag fee in the form of a coupon off future flights.

Once you find the baggage service desk, ask the clerk what to check on the baggage claim form or for the relevant form for expense reimbursement so they don't bounce your request later on a technicality. Save your receipts for items like makeup, socks, sun hat, sweater, hair spray, underwear, deodorant or whatever you purchase during the time your luggage is unavailable. These receipts may be required to get the reimbursement.

Most airlines practice stonewalling, and most people requesting compensation for their out-of-pocket expenses or even totally lost luggage are met with the outrageous demands of 'proof' for every item in the luggage. The Department of Transportation requires airlines to compensate passengers for provable loss up to $3,300 per passenger for domestic flights and $1,742 for international. If the airline is being uncooperative or has disallowed necessary expenses, go to www.dot.gov/airconsumer to fill out an online complaint. If that has no effect, filing in small claims court, which can cost between $25 and $75, often prompts them to settle with you.

Falling luggage. I'm always non-plussed at the random items people put in the overhead bins. One would expect a tidy row of wheeled bags and duffels. Loose items like a six pound computer tipped at an angle between two bags may tumble out when the bin is opened—and guess what, if you are the person clicking opening the bin, you are legally liable for injury to other passengers.

Not the airline. Not the owner of the item. You. The injured passenger sues you. The guy whose belonging was wrecked by the fall sues you. There are lawyers who specialize in this lucrative niche. When you open that bin, do it slowly and have the other hand at the ready to brace against any stray item inclined to fall out.

TSA Scanners

First off, skip complaining about the odious procedures until you get home; when in the airport and airplane, zip it. If you haven't flown for awhile, before going through security checks, watch a couple of other people go through it. Observe what the agents send them back to remove (watches, belts), and learn from the swift routines of the experienced travelers. Then go forward in a good mood and guilt-free spirit.

If you're bringing anything unusual, such as a prototype, industrial part, machine, equipment, or a lot of metal and corded items, don't wait for the hassle to descend upon you. Just put it in a bin all by itself. It's their job to question suspicious stuff going into the cabin. The least hassle is to have that discussion when no concealment was demonstrated.

The things most likely to cause the TSA staff to request you open your bag so they may take a closer look are

1) hidden liquids containers

2) small electronics, things with cords or batteries

3) things made of metal

4) big shoes.

For the least hassle, even if it's not required, put plastic and metal containers, empty or full, into the tub with your shoes, wallet, pocket items, belt or purse. You are allowed to bring empty containers through, but you do yourself no favors if you hide them.

Electronics / metal items. Put everything with a battery, cord, charger, or having a solid metal exterior or metal blade-like parts into a clear bag (no size requirements on this) and drop it into the tubs too. Mystery solved. When scanning, they view the items from one angle, and even common items can cast an unusual shadow when balled up with other items.

Bundling up the cords and powered items isn't mandatory; it just makes it easier for the TSA, who then makes it easier on you.

Lastly, shoes with thick soles or bulky heels often warrant a second look.

TSA will want to look at the shoes in your luggage, in both checked bags and carry-on.

It goes without saying, but I'll say it: making jokes about having a bomb, asking why they think you have a bomb or gun, or in general using the words 'terrorist' 'bomb' 'explosive' 'gun' and you get it, while in an airport is ill-advised. There is no possibility of being funny; they've heard it before.

Also don't get vocal about how stupid or scientifically unsupported these measures are. They hear it all day, and it makes you a pill. Pills don't get the benefit of the doubt when they need it.

Simply don't say it and don't try to be funny or witty about the state of TSA security measures. It will cause you to have a much lengthier experience with TSA.

One of the TSA staff may talk to you. It's a test. They are looking for inappropriate responses that indicate a guilty conscience like hostility, over-the-top efforts to be funny, large gestures, quarrelsomeness or refusal to say anything, as if you've already been read your Miranda rights. Simply respond appropriately, whatever that is. Laugh politely at their joke, say OK. Press lips together if asked to open your bag, sigh deeply if made to remove more stuff and go through the people scanner again, but don't go ballistic. Act normal, which can encompass not being happy about being inconvenienced.

They speak to you simply to hear your voice: is it nervous or scared? Are you thrown for a loop by the question "Where are you headed today?" Do you have trouble concentrating or slur your words? They get it that some people don't speak the language or have a bad stutter, but respond in your normal fashion when someone asks you a question.

They are looking for congruence. If you are nervous because it's the first time you're going through the TSA scanners in your life, say "I haven't flown in twenty years, this is my first airport scanner." Sharing the reason for excessive nervousness or anxiety is a timesaver. Telling strangers about your major concern is well-balanced, normal behavior. "I must seem a wreck, but my brother is in intensive care and may be gone by the time I get there." That would explain the about-to-cry look glued to your face. Congruence. The TSA is looking for congruence, not a specific set of behaviors. High-strung, nervous people do not get more hassle; most of us can tell when people are always like that.

George Orwell once said "By forty, every man has the face he deserves." Or may it was fifty. At any rate, after twenty-two we are all on the road to earning the face we deserve. When your face is congruent with your behavior, even if you're normally a touchy, smart-alecky hot-head, you might breeze through the TSA scanners despite all that. But please, if not for yourself, then for the sake of the people behind you, give it a rest.

Polite requests. This leads nicely to another point, receiving a very calm, gentle request from TSA officers, flight attendants, or airport staff. Don't make them ask twice.

Different families have different customs, and in your family this sort of 'please put that dish in the sink' tone may have neither compelling urgency nor crushing repercussion for non-compliance. This is not mom, and some of these requests have prison terms for two minute delays.

Tone of voice cannot be the deciding factor in whether you will commence complying in a few seconds or keep doing what you're doing for another minute.

All the airport/airline employees are trained to use a nice tone of voice regardless of the nature of the request. By doing this they do not alarm or draw the attention of nearby people. They allow you to retain your dignity while getting reined in or guided.

When asked to sit down, turn off your electronics, put on your seatbelt, stay in line, come over here, or other small direction or request, ignoring it can end up with you in handcuffs if you think you'll do that later on, not right now.

Sometimes you will be asked to do something that is puzzling or might indicate they misunderstand your situation. It is OK to ask for clarification or explain your situation again. If you still don't understand, the real question becomes whether it takes less time to do what you are asked than keep grilling them about it. If it's no big deal to you, won't have lasting repercussions that ruin your day or even the next hour, then simply comply without understanding. The only reason to continue to protest would be because it impacts your health, would ruin your travel plans, or another serious repercussion affecting hours, not just the next ten minutes.

It could be important. This goes back to the first thing, the seriousness of noncompliance could be far out of proportion to their tone of voice or urgency.

Instead of speculating on what kinds of reasons could prompt it, if you are asked nicely to move over there, open your bag, drop that umbrella, leave the restroom, let these men come through or other instruction by a quiet-voiced uniformed staffer with an I'm-not-joking look on his or her face, do it with as much haste as if they had an Uzi on their hip.

Jet Lag

The best way to handle jet lag on trips over four hours is to force yourself to follow the day at the destination time zone. North-South flights do not cause jet lag when less than two time zones were crossed. Anyone who says they have jet lag when flying from New York to Chile has either napped too much during the day or didn't sleep at all during the night while on the plane.

The 1 PM Rule works for flights going in either direction. If your landing time is before 1 PM, nap on the plane. If your landing time is after 1 PM, do not sleep on the plane and stay awake as much as you can.

Either way, go to bed no earlier than 7 PM that first night. By the second day bedtime can rotate to 9 or 11 PM, or your usual bedtime.

A general rule for short flights, when you're in the air for under three hours, is to stay awake. Nap only if you didn't catch enough winks the night before.

The 1 PM rule was written by a flight attendant, and I've been trying to poke holes in it for two years. So far, it's perfect.

Most US to Europe flights, even with a stopover somewhere, land between 5 AM and late morning. So grab every possible minute of sleep on the flights over. Drifting off at 4 or 6 PM once you sit down on the plane is less hard than you imagine, because the night before you will get next to no sleep. You're primed to doze off.

They serve a dinner and play a movie. Skip those. You just sleep. Who the heck eats dinner at 2 AM and watches a movie at 3 AM? That's what you're doing if you land at 8 AM and ate their goofus meal six hours ago.

The return flight is a different story: watch movies, start conversations, read, play games.

For a flight heading East, or from the US to Europe:

Ear plugs or noise cancelling headphones
Eye shades or hat over the face
Neck pillow
Coat, sweater, airline-provided blanket or all three
Support socks (if over 40)
Ibuprofen
Sleep aid (read on for tips)
Water bottle (filled or purchased after the scanners)

For a flight traveling with the sun or points West, i.e. home:

Caffeine gum, energy strips, five hour energy bottle, etc.
Interesting book, Kindle, Sudoku, games, movies stored on
    your phone
Ibuprofen
Support socks (if over 40)
Water bottle (filled or purchased after the scanners)

Details:

For water, use a sturdy bottle, such as a soda or iced tea bottle instead of a flimsy water bottle. These hold up better if you forget to let it 'breathe' when landing, and are less likely to spring a hole if roughly handled, such as pinched in the seatback magazine pocket while half full.

Accept the little pillow the airline hands out even if you brought a neck pillow. The armrests are often hard and cut off circulation over time. The airline's pillow can pad the armrest between passengers.

If you do not put on eyeshades or put the hat over your face, the flight attendant or your seatmate WILL poke you at mealtime, poke again to see if you want to buy a headset, and poke again to ask if you want a juice. Just closing your eyes with a blanket snugged to your chin won't stop it. You will get so pissed you won't be able to fall back asleep. Wear eyeshades or a hat over the face as an announcement, not because you need to.

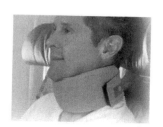

Neck pillow, the Embrace collar, available on Amazon.com. Wrapped around a purse strap or belt loop in the airport, it doesn't count toward weight limits.

Earplugs are a significant help in blurring the noise so you can sleep through all the unfamiliar sounds. People have different ear canal sizes so select a pair that fit your ears and are still comfortable six hours later. Noise-cancelling headphones work for some people.

I put my water bottle, which is really a repurposed iced tea bottle, in the seat pocket. When I half-wake because my mouth has become so dry I can't swallow, I'm able to wave about, land on the bottle, and take a drink without removing the eyeshades. Luxury.

The airplane meal is no big loss. You are going to ITALY! The place with the most delectable food and bakery. Landing and being hungry and ready for a Sfogliatella, cantucci, coffee and biscotti; how great is that?

On the way back it might seem like a good plan is to watch the in-flight movie to keep yourself awake, but that often doesn't start for an hour, and on long flights with two movies there could be an hour between them. So bring other interesting stuff to do, or talk politics with your seatmate.

Walking around. Easier said than done. It can seem the airlines do all in their power to discourage it, including using the food cart to prevent passage. Ugh, don't get me started talking about airline beverage service . . . every time I fly I mentally start designing a better cart and beverage service.

I've been a motion-reduction expert, implementing lean manufacturing, process improvement and waste reduction all my life. It's in my bones.

When I was only sixteen, the other girls in my gym class noticed how fast I changed and asked me to show them how to do it. In a few weeks the gym teacher mused that all the other classes needed six minutes to change, but this one was dressed and ready in two minutes. It's simple, really; standardize the sequence, eliminate the non-value-adding motions and create a good left-hand, right-hand procedure.

When I see every airline persist in serving a drink with the maximum wasted motions humanly possible year in and year out, it must be intentional. They want to block the aisle for the entire trip and make busywork for their staff. Any lean expert could improve this. Airlines just don't want to; I suspect the ritual they have serves as an additional security check. It isn't about serving a beverage; like the TSA, it's about looking you in the eye and asking a question.

The beverage cart is a very risky design. There are many tales about pinched fingers, wounded feet, damaged elbows and terrible lacerations from runaway carts. It's an awful vehicle for narrow aisles and poor visibility. If you have an aisle seat, protruding limbs are at risk. The flight attendants drive the cart up and down the aisle without looking—poor visibility makes that impossible—or they drag it backwards. If they hit your foot, knee or elbow, it will hurt. The cart may go up and down the aisles several times per flight. All things considered, it would be nice if a staffer led the way, gently shoving aside all feet and hands and children aside whenever the cart moved. Wishful thinking.

Carts today weighs too much. If the airplane angles up or down and the cart starts moving, the average flight attendant doesn't have the body mass to stop it. All she can do is scream and hope no one gets hurt. At the very least, why doesn't it have cow-catcher features on both ends so stray arms and knees are nudged aside?

My design concept is a beverage cart similar to a two-wheeled golf bag carrier, one for hot, one for cold and one for beer/wine. The handle would have a 1.25 inch hole. Every third seatback would have a one inch diameter pin, two inches high. The handle hole would drop onto the pin, serve, serve, move to next pin. If it becomes a runaway, it falls down and lays there. At under fifty pounds, the flight attendant has a fighting chance of holding it. One-handed, fail-safe, and won't fully block an aisle. Cup-holders on the top allow common drinks like coffee and orange juice to be poured four at a time, then simply handed out. Only at the end of the line would they begin pouring one at a time.

But I digress. We were talking about your trip . . .

On falling asleep

Sitting up on a plane, heading toward parts unknown with tight leg space beside dozens of strangers is just not conducive to the total abandonment of heedfulness that sleep requires.

It must be helped along. Don't expect to do it 'naturally.' There is nothing natural about being 36,000 feet in the sky in a metal box with total strangers. Natural doesn't come into play here. Be fair.

Melatonin works for many people. Antihistamines that make you drowsy are good too. Dramamine® motion sickness medication does the trick for many people. To quiet the little discomforts that awaken you after an hour, take ibuprofen.

When you wake up sometime after three or four hours with a dry mouth, have some more ibuprofen handy in a pocket to swallow along with the few swigs from your water bottle. For myself, a dose of ZzzQuil, Berry flavor, before leaving home, which was three hours before the flight, worked great. My earlier testing found when taken at 10 PM, it didn't cause drowsiness before midnight, yet it prevented that wide-awake feeling six hours later at 4 AM and left me with a strong urge to sleep until 8:30. That's what I wanted. Something that permitted me to eke out that last hour of sleep. I controlled the bright-eyed wake-up moment by controlling the swallow time.

Test sleep aids and stay-awake aids ahead of time! You could discover a tame over-the-counter sleep aid works so well on you that six hours later you're still groggy, not walking straight or answering questions sensibly. You don't want that. Taking half a pill might work.

Conversely, you may find the energy shot gives you diarrhea five hours later. Not good. Who wants to be behind the wheel in rush hour traffic when a restroom is needed in the next five minutes?

Children get the opposite effect from many stimulant or relaxing drugs; coffee makes them drowsy and Dramamine can make them more alert; the occasional adult retains that effect. A good example of this is ADHD medication; in children under ten it appears to be a sedative, making hyperactive children more calm; the same medication will make a twenty year old able to study through the night with a ton of energy. Your biology, ancestry, age, weight, other drugs, diet and vitamin levels all have an effect on what works for you at what dosage. There are five different antacid chemicals on the market and they all work—for some people.

No pill or potion for sleep or wakefulness works for everyone; if a brand name works for even 40% of people, they have a steady enough clientele to stay in business.

Non-drug techniques help too; get up a few hours earlier than normal so you're ready for a long nap by 6 PM. If you sleep on the plane, you'll arrive in Italy at breakfast-time after six and a half hours of sleep and ready for a full day starting with a coffee. The travelers who ate the meals and watched a movie are going to bed, and will feel messed up for three days.

Ear adjustment to pressure.

Everyone is different, and there's no telling who has big wide Eustachian tubes that normalize the pressure behind the ear drum quickly and who doesn't. The Eustachian tubes are two normally closed, seldom-used tubes running from the back of the throat to each ear, into the pocket behind the ear drum. The purpose is for swimming, so our eardrums don't burst every time we go below 14 feet of water, which is 20.7 psi. Water depth psi is way more dramatic than the tiny psi differences on a plane.

Sometimes there is no pain, just an odd deafness. This usually goes away in a few hours, or you can speed it along using #6 below.

It's inevitable a first-time flyer is going to have some ear pressure discomfort. Here's a plan of attack. If you find other advice, by all means give it a shot. The bottom line is, do what works for you because everyone is different. The more you fly, the less you suffer from this.

1) Take ibuprofen about one to three hours before landing, so it's in full effect. It's mandatory for babies and small children. I'm puzzled why airlines don't sell liquid ibuprofen for babies right next to the glass of wine on the cart.

2) Stress, or focusing on your ears can cause them to tighten up. Distract yourself with a crossword puzzle, Sudoku, practicing your Italian, whatever serves to distract you. Being asleep is good too.

3) Chew gum. Work the jaw and swallow, wiggle that Eustachian tube around until it lets some air through.

4) Yawn. Or just pretend to yawn, same thing.

5) Some people say the kind of antihistamines that open air passages also open Eustachian tubes.

6) When discomfort starts heading into pain, you can force air into the low-pressure cavity by pinching your nose tightly closed, then blowing your nose as hard as you can until you hear a squeak and one ear feels fine. Repeat as needed.

7) Pinched your nose and blew, but only helped one ear? Sometimes, pinch/blow while plugging the good ear very firmly with your finger will cause the air to go to the still-hurting ear. Worth a shot.

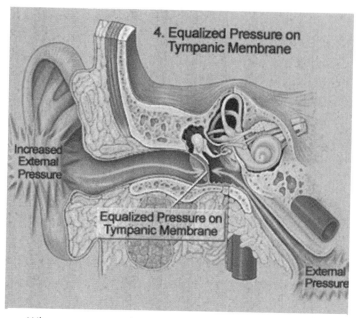

When ears start to hurt upon landing, pinch nose closed, take a breath and then 'blow your nose.' With luck a bit of air will go up the Eustachian tube of the worst ear for instant relief.

PACKING

Pack light by not packing for 'a trip.'

Instead, look at your itinerary and envision what you'll be doing each day. From that, decide what to wear that day.

This clarifies whether you can get by with one pair of shoes or need three, or if it's worthwhile to bring pajamas or a sweatsuit. A woman doing ordinary tourist activities for a week might find that a pair of jeans and a skirt with pockets covers the situation pretty well. Or perhaps just two pairs of pants.

Packing light is about predicting yourself. If you get a handle on the typical weather and your typical activities, every piece carried will come home as dirty laundry. Pack no just-in-case clothing. In August, take no sweater. In March, take no t-shirt. If you find you'd like to wear one, buy it.

If you don't break it down by day, it's possible to pack three dresses and two pairs of heels for a trip that contains only one fine dining experience. You and your spouse may be open to the fun of sleeping in just your underwear on this trip, but if it includes two nights at a distant relative's home, packing modest nightwear is necessary. Without a plan that gives equal weight to each day, it's easy to overpack for the activity that looms large in your imagination and underpack for the normal activities of the other days.

Another approach is to select and put on one complete outfit, shoes, socks, jewelry and all, that is comfortable, weather appropriate, and you could see yourself wearing for fifteen hours straight in museums and churches and walking for five miles. Strip and toss into the carry-on. Grab some spare underwear and socks. Done.

Well, not really. Clothes get sweaty, you sit on something, some days will be a little colder, or a little hotter . . . so add a second complete outfit, plus a third top. Begrudge every additional item.

In today's casual environment, most men and women could get by wearing jeans every day. No one expects jeans to be washed after every wearing, and most people look pretty good in them. Capris jeans could be just about the perfect summer-in-Italy wear for women.

The hardest part of packing light is the mental adjustment, the urge to pack for just-in-case because dragons-be-there, it's so new and different. Perhaps it will be, but not in regards to clothes, your body, and weather. Those will be old friends. Comfort, not wishful thinking, is the direction to lean when packing.

Even on a tight budget, consider packing less clothing than you need and buying it in Italy. In Rome, between the Ottaviano subway station and the Vatican, open air shops sell breezy skirts and tops for €10 to cover the elbows and knees of unprepared tourists. Booths have amazing deals on €2 earrings and €5 silk bags. In Florence, the leather goods—wallets, purses, belts—cost 30% of their US price, so a tight budget is all the more reason to buy a five year supply plus a couple of birthday presents ahead of time.

Appropriate dress. Touristy places in warm climates are so accustomed to the casual wear of people on vacation that you won't feel out of place in jeans and a polo shirt or khakis and a striped top even in expensive restaurants. A single nice outfit will suffice no matter how many fancy events call for it over the span of two weeks. To everyone you meet it's the first time you're wearing it, as far as they know or care.

The airline limitations aren't the reason to travel light. As of this writing, most airlines allow one free checked bag for overseas flights weighing up to fifty pounds. You never want to get even remotely close to topping out on the way there because you'll collect ten pounds of souvenirs, new clothes, receipts and brochures during the trip.

The big reason to travel light is because you have to carry every bit of it multiple times all by yourself, up and down stairs, ramps, over puddles and up into trains, buses or car trunks. No matter how nice the wheels on the thing, Italy doesn't cooperate. Skinny stairways, cobblestones, high curbs, steep ramps, mud, and gaps that need to be hopped are standard daily fare.

If you're a woman thinking "I can bring what I like, my husband will carry it," my answer to that is, if he can't manage all of it in one trip but continually needs to make two trips while you stand guard on the half-moved stuff, your vacation will be marred by snafus. If the load is so onerous and unwieldy that he pulls a muscle on the third day, your wonderful Italy vacation will be curtailed for both of you. When traveling, the saying 'pull your own weight' can be taken literally. If you want to bring more stuff, get some eight pound barbells and start working them.

How to Meet the Weight Requirements by Cheating

Part of packing light can be done by cheating. Wear all your heaviest clothes to the airport, even two or three tops, and remove them in the restroom before boarding or once you get on the plane.

Put some heavy things in your pockets before approaching the airport with its bag-weighing stations. When you get to the scanners, simply empty your pockets, like you're supposed to, into the tub. On the other side, who cares if those items go back into the pockets or into the carry-on? Obviously this won't work for twelve pounds of stuff, but it's feasible to fudge two or even four pounds this way.

Some airlines have weighing stands at the gate too. If you spot equipment for weighing bags at the gate, keep the heavy pocket stuff in your pockets until you're on the plane.

A new trend is wearable luggage. The idea is you wear several more items of clothing that you normally do, and buy their jacket or vest with many pockets to store spare shoes, unmentionables, and toiletries. Time will tell if this gets popular, but based on the early-stage wearable-luggage items I saw, there's plenty of room for improvement in the garment.

I am a big fan of good, large-size pockets in travel clothes. Pants with dinky pockets that barely hold a crumpled tissue can be taken to a tailor to get new, deep pockets that can hold a cell phone plus passport, pen and travel pack of tissue. Each. This works really well with jeans and khakis.

Consider taking an article of clothing you like to a tailor to have an interior pocket added, in lieu of using a money belt. Selecting and buying the pocket material yourself and bringing it with the garment to the tailor means you have a little more control over color and thickness. Tip: cut a piece of cardboard to the largest size object you want to slip in and out and fit nicely within, and give it to the tailor for sizing the pocket.

There are vests with many pockets. They're called fishing vests and they're available for both men and women. In practice, vests are unflattering, sweaty, yet don't keep you warm. A problem with fishing vests is the pockets may not be the size you need.

Whether vest or deeper pockets, at the TSA scanners the vest will need to be taken off and dropped into a bin. Clothes pocket items also go into the bins. The vest can travel through with all contents unless they ask to see something.

Another way to cheat is to decide to visit a Profumeria the same day you land, to buy hair spray, mousse, lotion, shampoo, even deodorant. One and two-star hotels often don't provide shampoo, but three stars do, so if your first night hotel is a three star or up, see what amenities they provide before you go shopping.

The other way to cheat is to decide to buy all your clothes there, and bring only underwear. Italy has perfectly nice clothes, lovely clothes, and whatever you buy will probably be more stylish that what you'd bring. Buying clothes in America before a trip to Italy is truly bringing coals to Newcastle.

Ponte Vecchio at sunset. The bridge is lined with small shops in the heart of Florence. It's one of the most photographed bridges in Italy. It was built in the 1500s to connect the town hall with Palazzo Pitti on the other side of the river. Since 1593 the shops have been confined, by law, to goldsellers and dealers of small valuables.

What to Pack

Bring what looks good on you, is comfortable and is appropriate for the weather. You will be taking many photos; this isn't the time to tie your hair back, go make-up-less, or wear old t-shirts. Dress the way you want to look for posterity.

Mix and match? If you wear exactly the same top with the same bottom every other day for ten days, there's no downside. If you like the outfit and it flatters you, it doesn't have to go with any other thing in the luggage.

Consider polyester. Polyester tops hang attractively, never wrinkle, weigh less and stain less. The thin ones can be cooler than cotton in hot weather and don't show sweat like cotton does.

Cotton isn't always the best for travel. Cotton changes color when wet, gets clammy, gets stinky, gets salt stains from sweat that are hard to get out. There are better breathable, quicker-drying shirt materials out there.

The toiletries bag and shoes are going to be the big items. Select their positions, then work the rest around them.

Vacuum bags. The idea is that all the air is squeezed out of several items of clothes, making them fit in a smaller space. This is a better idea for a one-destination trip or a cruise, not a package tour or self-guided tour when you repack for a new hotel every two days. The weight is still there. If the bag gets nicked by the zipper or gets a hole, there goes the advantage. I'm a fan of stuffing items into a smaller container. But these things are time-consuming and finicky to roll up, and you just may not have the time.

Water bottle. This can be brought along with you through the scanners as long as it's empty. After the scanners, fill it at a drinking fountain. Put it right in the bin or keep it on the outside of your carry-on, don't hide it inside your luggage. Choose a sturdy bottle, such as a soda or iced tea bottle instead of a flimsy water bottle. These hold up better if you forget to let it 'breathe' when landing, and are less likely to spring a hole if roughly handled, such as pinched in the seatback magazine holder while half full.

In addition to providing drinking water during the flight, if you outfit it with a clip or loop for attaching to a belt loop or your purse strap, it helps on hot days that don't involve museum or church visits. Keep it by the bed to wet your whistle at night.

Bottoms

Start your packing plan with bottoms. Rather than use different language for men and women, the word 'bottoms' covers whatever you have between waist and knees that shows, at least partially, to the public. Bottoms consist of pants, jeans, shorts, skirts, dresses, crop pants, leggings, capris pants and kilts. Bottoms dictate the shoes and socks needed. In addition to what you wear on the plane, have one bottom maximum for every three days with a four-bottom maximum. Pack one bottom for a four-day trip, two for a seven-day trip, three for a ten-day trip. If each bottom requires a different footwear, rethink. Ideally, all bottoms go with the shoes you wear to the airport. That is often a bit too ideal, so pack a second pair of footwear or buy some when you get there. I regret talking myself out of buying a pair of gondola shoes in Venice.

Loose capris with elastic waist work with any event and go with any footwear; sneakers, heels, sandals.

I said no one needed to buy new clothes to pack light, but I am going to make a suggestion for women. Capris like these, with elastic waist and polyester fabric that never wrinkles, can go from mountain hike to city tour to beach to church to fancy restaurant with a change of top and shoes. It goes with running shoes, sandals, and heels. Most vacation travelers could get by with one pair of jeans and one pair of these for ten days or more.

Pack bottoms by rolling them up. Fold the two legs together, then roll up starting with the waist. Or vice versa, doesn't matter. Skirts and dresses can be folded into thirds and rolled up, or rolled up without folds for a smaller-diameter but longer item.

Shoes. Ideally, all shoes are ten-hour shoes. Sneakers (encompasses all manner of sports shoe) or boat shoes make good primary shoes. If the main shoes are starting to rub or cause a blister, the back-up shoes can be brought into play. Sandals, flip-flops or ballet slipper styles may be good backup shoes for women, sandals for men, assuming it's between April and October. If there will be fine dining or formal events, regular leather shoes may need to be the

Street heels for evening wear, if you must bring high heels

backup. Wedge heels, not spike heels, work the best on Italy's cobblestone streets and sidewalks.

In the airport the TSA will want to look at shoes with heels in your luggage, whether checked or carry-on. Be prepared to open it. Put nothing inside of shoes that you wouldn't mind a stranger handling in public.

Face the shoes to each other toe to heel, or mirror-image with soles touching, or stuff the toe of one into the other--play around until you find the smallest space. To keep them tight, use the big rubber band from celery, asparagus or other veggie. An option for large or heavy shoes is to place one on each side of the luggage, sole to the outside, or even sole up, facing the lid. The other items will bear against the leather upper. If they might get dirty later on, put each in a plastic bag.

Slippers. Or fluffy fleece socks or flip-flops. Rubber-soled beach shoes work too. Don't walk around barefoot on strange-to-you floors; things buried in the carpet, cords not against the wall, slightly raised carpet nails, unseen sharp edges on tiles and carpet edgers can cause momentary pain if not actually break the skin. Wear something on your feet.

Tops

Like bottoms, tops encompass what either sex wears between shoulders and belly button and displays at least partially to the world. Tops are where your personal style and taste evinces itself. When packing, fold them in half or thirds and roll them up too. If you stand your rolls on end, it's possible to have total access to all clothes without disturbing anything else, eliminating the need to unpack.

Pack one top per day minus two, for either the entire trip or up to the day you'll do laundry. It's not as generous as it sounds because sometimes you'll wear two of the tops. Regardless of weather, pack one short-sleeved or no-sleeved top that goes with at least one long-sleeved top, sweater or jacket you bring. Consider buying clothes in Italy. You get to wear them immediately and later on they remind you of this trip. How great is that? It's better to spend the money in Italy rather than poke through stores before the trip.

Sweater or overshirt. Pack one that is 80% or more synthetic, not cotton. A cotton sweater provides little to no warmth, changes color when wet, is heavy, and stains easily. Avoid cotton in clothing that is meant to add warmth, provide modesty or protect you from the elements. A sweater or fleece covers a wide range of conditions. In cooler weather a leather jacket might be better, keeping you sharp-looking and warm all day long.

Dress for cool temps on the plane in all seasons, but in warm climates also be prepared for a long hot wait on the tarmac. Planes do not have air conditioning when not moving. Having a tank top under your clothes can be handy if you're stuck for a spell on the tarmac.

While I recommend one top for each day of the trip, minus two, in practice I cheat. A t-shirt that will be used for exercise, worn under a regular shirt, or as a sleep top doesn't count toward the top count, it is 'underwear.'

Underwear

Put all underwear in cloth bags, such as the kind that come with liquor or shoes. Checked or carry-on, never use clear baggies for underwear. Scattering underwear into odd corners is even worse. Use cloth bags for dirty laundry too. When the TSA encounters a cloth bag, they manipulate it, feeling for hard items. If it's just all squishy clothes and obvious bra underwires, it passes. So mixing your sunglasses, spare batteries, souvenir belt buckles, candles or any other hard item in with (clean or dirty) underwear is an awful idea; it means the TSA may need to dump it all out on the TSA examining table and fish through your undies to check out the mystery item. Yuk!

How much underwear to bring? Your comfort level is the deciding factor. You have permission to overpack underwear if you like.

Women: one pair of underwear per day of trip length, up to nine. Trips under five days, only the bra worn. Over that, one more. Additional underwear garments for a specific occasion as needed. Some people swear that wearing an underwire bra through the TSA scanners causes hassle. I always wear underwire bras and never encountered a moment's delay by the TSA. Some people reply that many underwire bras these days have plastic, not wires, and I must be unknowingly buying those. Fair enough. I'm not taking one apart to find out. My opinion, which counts for something because I designed an airport baggage X-ray scanner, is that the scanner programming has code that ignores underwire bras on people having female proportions. This is a feasible programming task.

A silky polyester red, dark blue or black robe can do triple duty as sleepwear, bathrobe, swimsuit cover, and even become a light wrap if you feel cold. It slides on quickly when there's a knock on the door. It balls up small and never wrinkles. The ones at Macy's have two generous pockets.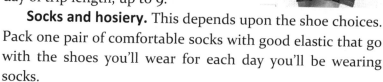

Men: One pair of underwear per day of trip length, up to 9.

Socks and hosiery. This depends upon the shoe choices. Pack one pair of comfortable socks with good elastic that go with the shoes you'll wear for each day you'll be wearing socks.

If the elastic gives out during the trip and they become annoying or develop holes, don't hesitate to throw them out; don't carry them a minute longer, they will never get better. If you intend to do laundry in the middle, pack enough socks to reach that day.

Socks are a poor candidate for sink washing. Consider simply airing them out for a day, talcum-powdering them and wearing them again.

If there will be any occasion that must have nylons, pack two pair, at least one of them unused in the package.

Immediately after putting them on in the hotel, slide on the shoes, slippers, or pair of socks. The main cause of snags or tears is stepping on something imperceptible in the carpet or a sharp edge on a tile. If you have no clear occasion for nylons but might use them, pack one pair.

Hat, eyeshades. Between April and November, bring a sun hat or baseball cap. Even if it isn't your normal habit. A hat is a bit of personal shade. Believe it or not, the sun beating on the top of your head is a primary cause of sunstroke, or of feeling queasy from the heat.

On the plane, nothing says "Leave me alone" like a baseball cap or hat pulled down over the face. I like eyeshades, which accomplish the same thing, but many people can't stand them. When it isn't too hot it's cold, and a hat can help keep you warm.

For women, a hat can be freeing; it covers a bad hair day and custom permits her to leave it on all day. In fact, women wearing a hat into a church is considered a sign of respect. The hat is also good for rain or drizzle. The hat could be kept in the daybag until needed, or clipped to a belt.

All you need for phone and computer chargers. Fine for dual voltage blow dryers too.

Electrical Devices. In Italy the adapter with three prongs is needed. Other European countries with 50 Hz, 240V electrical service accept the two-prong kind, but in Italy those might work at only 30% of places. Check the tiny fine print on your phone charger, computer brick, and other appliances you wish to bring. Trust the plug. If it says 100V-240V and 50-60 Hz, believe it. For these you only need the very light plug adapter, not the much heavier converter. I recommend the OREI Grounded Universal two in one Plug Adapter Type L for Italy; it allows two items at right angles at the same time.

Travel voltage converters don't have a good track record, tending to burn up. They can't manage blow dryers, hair curlers, and in some cases rechargeable shavers. Computers don't need them.

No matter what anyone tells you or you read elsewhere, you need the three-prong, not two-prong, adapter in Italy.

A computer. Think hard whether you can skip this by loading your Favs and docs onto a USB stick to use with hotel or library computers, or installing apps on your phone and bring only a light Bluetooth keyboard and a pair of reading glasses to do what you need to with Word and Excel on the phone. Test opening and saving attachments to emails, etc. while at home.

A waterproof watch. This is useful even if you usually get the time from your phone. So many things are time sensitive that having the local time right there, to check like a nervous Nellie every ten minutes if you want, is a comfort. It can be laid on the counter in the bathroom so you can keep an eye on the time without touching your phone with wet hands. Really, never bring the phone into a hotel bathroom at all. You know . . . hard floors, wet, mist, towel, kerplunk, elbow, drip, spray, fumble, cra-a-a-k.

Wimpy, lukewarm breeze, standard equipment in Italy. Bring your own hair dryer if you don't have short hair.

Blow dryer. Many hotels provide the apparatus shown here, which produces a lukewarm breeze. It takes three times longer to dry hair with this than with a hot travel dryer having a switch for 120V or 240V.

The tiny Babyliss Pro is a good travel blow dryer. It weighs only ten ounces and dries hair as fast as the much bigger ones. Be scrupulous about setting the switch to the appropriate setting. Flip it to 240V at home before packing it so you don't whip it out and start using it while still set at 120V. My hunch is that people who say it died after a few minutes of use ran it for a few seconds or longer at the wrong setting, then flipped it and hoped that tiny bit didn't matter. It does.

A blow dryer can also warm up a cold bathroom and remove wrinkles from clothes.

Duct tape. Some travel tips folks really believe in this one, but I've never had it and never felt a need for it. However, there's no downside to bringing it. Don't bring the whole roll; rewind a yard or two around a toiletry item. Bluntly, the silver stuff is garbage; the Duck tape brand has better adhesive and comes in white, beige, red, well dozens of colors.

Toiletries bag

I am a huge fan of keeping it all in one place, meaning stashing all the small stuff in pockets and sleeves of one or two small bags. This can be a purchased item, but it doesn't have to be; an old purse or something with a few zipper pockets picked up at a rummage sale will suffice.

When you travel a lot you start getting particular, but when you aren't picky there are two considerations: 1) size 2) leak-proofness.

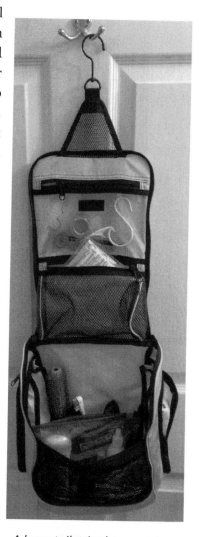

A large toiletries bag can store cords, batteries, liquids, medicines, brushes. . . basically every non-clothing item you bring along in one spot. Yellow instead of black improves visibility in dim bathrooms.

If it isn't inherently waterproof, ziploc baggies do the trick, solving any compartment or isolation needs too. As for size, you want it ample enough to fit everything in a loose fashion yet close easily and not dump things out.

The first decision point is: do you want to set it on the counter or hang it? For hanging it needs a hook or strap on top. If you prefer setting on the countertop or intend to keep it on the nightstand, then a container that parks well, like a man's toiletries leather bag or even a plastic kitchen storage container can work. The hanging kind is great in Europe where there is little counter space in bathrooms. Hang on any hook, knob or towel rack. If it has a loop, buy an 'S' hook at the hardware store. Often the towel rack is all there is.

One bag or two? Placing charging cords, medicines, and some odds and ends in a second bedside bag makes sense. I used two bags for many years, but now use one large bag. Electrical items go into the outside zipper pocket. My bag is large enough to just drop my quart bag of liquids into it.

A smaller bag means some items like hairbrush and mousse go in a gallon baggie. You want to bag anything in a spray bottle or with a twist-off lid. Movement and pressure changes make lids unscrew, caps come off, or press down on the sprayer. Within the baggie it might be a mess, but at least your clothes and other things are fine. Be scrupulous in Ziploc-bagging every liquid, spray or cream every time it gets tucked away, even into a drawer. Don't do it only when you think there's a risk, because naturally it only happens when you don't think it will.

Anything you might want while your traveling companion is in the shower, like ibuprofen, sugar substitute, antacid, inhaler or a cardboard nail file goes in the bedside bag.

One advantage to using a small bag is that it can be shoved into the room's safe when you leave. Don't bother imagining what someone might take. Don't give it a thought, just lock it up. If there is no safe, put it in a drawer, cover with clothing, or hide it in a piece of locked luggage. That doesn't seem like much of a safeguard, but the difference between being visibly tempting vs. not even knowing it's there unless one hunts around is huge. If there's nothing valuable, leave it hanging in the bathroom the entire stay.

Hand Sanitizer. Packing a tiny bottle is fine, but even better is buying a box of individually wrapped sanitizer towelettes. The packets do not need to go into your liquids bag. You can keep the main stash in your luggage and bring three to four in your fannypack or purse. They make a great little cover cloth if you have to touch something unsavory in a public place. Use one to wash your face after a long flight to look better. If you get a cut, not only will one clean it, but it catches the blood until you can make other arrangements. On a hot day, it's great to wipe the neck and ears to cool off fast. If you're grabbing a gelato in a cone after activities involving hand rails or handling items, you can wipe down your hands so you don't feel guilty licking your fingers. I've used them to clean gunk off my shoe and to steady a table with a short leg. I'm a big fan of the individually packaged sanitizer wipes.

Alcohol. Liquor in bottles under 3.4 oz. may be included in the liquids bag. These can be the regular mini-liquor bottles available at any liquor store, or the liquor of your choice can be poured into any liquids-appropriate container under 3.4 oz. Reusing liquid medication antacid, cold or cough medicine bottles reduces hassle. I bring Bailey's Hazelnut crème liquor to use as creamer in tea and coffee since it doesn't need refrigeration and I dislike powder creamer.

Tip: be discreet when making your own mixed drink on the plane. Not covert, just don't draw attention. To be legal, the rule is the liquor is to be handed to the flight attendant so he or she can make the drink, and hope they are as cognizant of the rules as you are so it will not be confiscated. Or, you could simply pour 'cough medicine' into orange juice after the serving attendant has moved three rows down and no one is looking.

Talcum powder. Take a tip from the deep south when traveling to hot weather locations: talcum powder under your clothes.

A sprinkle inside the bra keeps it from getting sweaty and clammy. It can be a substitute for deodorant if wearing a white shirt. Marathon runners put baby powder between the butt cheeks, where hours of motion can cause chafing. This happens to tourists too. A little talcum powder rubbed all over the feet before putting them into socks reduces chances of blisters, rashes and other foot ills. A great side effect is that your dirty laundry bag will not have as pungent an odor after five days. I find even the travel size baby powder is too big for most trips, so I transfer some to an even smaller bottle. I put this smaller bottle in my liquids bag for the TSA scanners just to reduce any possibility of hassle.

Small rubberbands or hair ties can serve as pants button extenders, as long as the shirt is left hanging out. Stick halfway thru buttonhole, then hook both ends over the button. It 'forgives' that big meal or three.

Makeup. Pack only one of each item, don't duplicate what you carry in your purse. This seems tough but really makes it easier. The exception would be anything that would really ruin your week if it were lost or damaged somehow. This is true of everything: travel light, but within reason. Have back-ups for anything that is really important to you. My lipstick shade and brand is really important to my confidence and comfort, so I bring two. Move things like face cream into a smaller, lighter container holding perhaps three days' more than you need. At the end of the trip some containers can be discarded rather than brought home.

Razor. Bring your usual one. If you're used to a Venus razor but pack a BIC disposable in the spirit of traveling light, the different shower layout combined with the un-familiar cutting tool will draw blood. The same goes for men. That little bit of weight is not worth dealing with annoying cuts.

Toothbrush. Bring your usual one, even if, no, especially if it's the battery-operated kind. There will be enough strangeness; your teeth need their usual, customary care. Buy a travel-size toothpaste. And no, you cannot bring an almost-empty large toothpaste tube; it risks hassle with TSA. They have decided a half-full larger container does not meet the 3.4 oz. limits, and are rigid to a goofy extent.

Facial tissue in travel packs is actually a toilet paper substitute if needed. Busy museum facilities run out, and if you can use a stall no one else can use because you have brought your own, it saves time and allows you to cut ahead in line. Tissue is the kind of thing you don't need until you really need it—for a skinned knee, a nosebleed, or to use this restroom NOW instead of incur another ten minutes of wait or walk. I put a second one in the main bag in case I use up the first one early in the trip.

Small Just-in-Case items. It's nice to have a few, but don't get carried away. They have stores in Italy. Things can do double duty: a half roll of foam tape is also plain tape; a paper clip is a small wire that can be formed into a hook and used for a multitude of fastening purposes depending how you bend it.

Foam tape is also handy to cover glowing LEDs that are bothering you; securing a cabinet door that won't stay closed; binding items tightly together; even holding up socks that just won't stay up (the cloth side may need a safety pin helping out, and on the top, encircle your leg below the knee—if you're hairy, fold the sticky side onto itself to make a band out of it)

Fiber Tablets. Even if you've never had a problem with constipation before, vacation entails diet changes plus a lack of access to restroom facilities. It's likely your first encounter will be while traveling. The combination of more cheese and less water than you're used to could lead to the first time your intestines say 'no room for more' in that slightly queasy, indefinable lead-weight  way which puts you off your game in a manner you don't care to share with prying family members.

There are many regularity products out there, but Fiber Choice tabs do a fine job and travel well; eat two like mints after a meal or even as a nibble while waiting in line. They don't increase urgency like laxatives. Excessive straining during bowel movements can cause burst eye blood vessels and worsen any other circulation problem from ears to hemorrhoids, annoyances you don't want to bother with on this trip. Take a few chewy candies and dodge the bullet. I like the Berry Pomegranate for the chewiness; the others are more powdery.

Buy your choice of fiber a few weeks before the trip to try out. You don't want something that causes urgency, as in "I need a bathroom in the next five minutes or I'm going to have a laundry problem." Don't bring anything like that to Italy, because 70% of the day you won't have that kind of access to facilities.

Deodorant, shaving cream, lotions. Bring only tried and true, items you've tested weeks before the trip; vacation is not the time to switch these things.

Shampoo, hair spray, mousse. If you like the travel sizes, perfect. Any small bottle with a threaded cap that closes tightly can hold your shampoo. To keep the liquids bag manageable, it's possible to buy them after you arrive.

On a trip to Italy I decided to buy them in Rome. In Italy, pharmacies have a blinking green cross protruding from the building, but sell nothing but drugs. Hair care, skin lotions and deodorants are sold in a perfume store, a Profumeria. Even if the window is full of pricey bottles of fragrance, step in and there will be shelving with shampoo and mousse.

Ibuprofen is the traveler's friend. It makes sleeping in uncomfortable chairs possible, it makes sore feet bearable, it makes your functional day a little longer and your mood slightly better. Whether it is earaches, blisters, pinched fingers, sunburn, a bad bruise or losing a filling, it can help you bull through your vacation with some level of enjoyment until you return home. It has anti-blood-clot powers and swelling-reducing powers that acetaminophen (Tylenol) does not. Taking it before bedtime improves quality of sleep in strange beds that may be firmer than you're used to. Taking it before a tour improves stamina. It calms sore muscles, relieves headaches, and helps backaches. The pills are small and light and improve quality of life. Don't travel without them.

Liquid Ibuprofen. I travel with an unopened bottle of baby ibuprofen, the kind with an eyedropper inside. Babies tend to get ear infections when traveling, new parents are by definition inexperienced, so of course they don't see this coming. I had one too many plane, train or bus trips marred by a child in terrible pain. When it happens, I simply hand over the entire still-sealed bottle to the caretakers. It costs me $5, what a bargain.

Extra Items. Everyone has their own unique stuff. To make the point, I'll share my own, I admit, totally indulgent baloney I bring along. Feel free to make up your own indulgent stuff.

My own teabags and yellow packet sugar substitute, enough for three cups per day. I like my own tea made my own way, so I order tea in restaurants just for the hot water, then I use my own.

Mio lemonade flavor.

Plastic coffee mug, 16 oz., and in North America, a clip-type heating element for making tea. I despise the tiny cups provided in hotel rooms, and don't care much for Styrofoam either. I'll use the coffeemaker in the room if there is one. In Italy there is often a coffee/hot water station in a small room off the lobby.

Hazelnut Crème liquor in a cough medicine bottle. Related to above. Italy often provides only powdered creamer for tea drinkers. Plus two or three little liquor bottles, lemon rum, etc. My feet may not feel up to checking out the nightlife, but savoring a lemonade and rum with my piggies propped up on a pillow while clicking through TV channels to satisfy my curiosity about what Italians watch on TV. . .ah, it doesn't get better than this. Well, maybe there's room for improvement, but I'm in Florence a biscuit toss from Ponte Vecchio so it can't get too much better.

A half-circle memory foam pillow. I mash it into a zippered nylon bag (that came with something else) so it takes one-third the space. I like it. I sleep better with it.

Kindle and charger. I have the kind that can go a month between charges, but still I bring the charger.

An Embrace Sleep Collar for the plane. The seats don't recline enough, and with this my head never bobbles forward once, not ever.

Black Magic marker. I've always used it. I make signs or leave notes that are noticed, repair something black that is scratched, ink over an LED whose light is bothering me.

Bathroom clock.

A one-to-three electrical outlet adapter. Most hotels have only one convenient outlet, the rest are behind furniture. This prevents the most common cause of leaving a charger behind. I charge phone, laptop and Kindle on the desk or someplace where I can see everything, not one of them behind the chair.

Outlet adapter to plug everything in an obvious place, even if there's only one slot left.

Medication. Keep prescription medication in the original container for the plane flight. Liquid medication larger than the allowed 3.4 oz. size is permitted if it's in the prescription bottle or you have a note from your doctor. If the medicine needs to stay cold, place it in an insulated bag with frozen gel packs right out in the open, and tell the security screener. Putting prescription medication into smaller baggies, especially mood-changing or pain meds, can look suspicious. Reduce hassle by using only bottles with the name of the traveler on them.

Pack as much medication as you need, plus a few more days' worth at minimum. If it makes sense for you, after arrival split the medication up, some in your purse and the rest in your luggage. The idea is to reduce risk if 'something happens' and in my experience the risk between purse that goes everywhere with you and the bag left alone in the room is about fifty-fifty. If your estimation of risk is different, put the medication in the least risky place. If there's a room safe, that's a great place for your medications; carry two days' worth of medication in case you are waylaid for any reason.

Some countries may require special permission to bring certain medications across their border. To find out if your medication is an issue when traveling internationally, visit the Center for Disease Control and Prevention's website, www.cdc.gov/travel.

Vitamin C. Get more than your usual share of vitamin C while traveling to improve your resistance to picking up illnesses. Vitamin C is available in chewable tabs and as hard candy/cough lozenges, so you can take it any time, not just at meals.

Carmex is a wonderful little product that has 100 uses. It's sold in every Walgreens, CVS and RiteAID in the US. It works as effectively as an antibiotic on cuts, scrapes, rashes, hangnails and blisters. Because it's designed for use on mucous membranes, it works well on lip cuts, cold sores, mouth burns (from pizza hot from the oven), gum infections, and pretty much any mouth situation. It is effective for irritation on all other parts of the body. If you suffer from an insufficient toilet paper issue or irritation from walking, clean the area well and squeeze a lump onto some toilet paper and apply to the sore area. It may feel very warm for a few minutes, but that means it's working. It can heal this kind of sore in three hours that would otherwise take two days to feel better.

Travel scissors, the folding kind, are legal for carry-on. How well the rules are understood varies from day to day, by agent or airport. These are legal, and when folded up in the toiletries bag do not draw attention to themselves.

Contact wearers. Saline solution and eye drops are not included in the 3.4 oz. bottle requirement, and do not have to be contained within the liquids baggie. You still have to separate out the bottles and declare them during screening, but you can have a bigger bottle than 3.4 oz. To reduce hassle, print out the rule from the TSA webpage and bring along, in case your TSA screener is unaware of it.

Fragile items. Wrap and insulate them with clothing at the center of your bag. Don't place them in a corner or edge; make sure every side, top and bottom has padding between item and suitcase wall.

First Aid

Your main first aid tools are Carmex, adhesive bandages, foam tape, ibuprofen, antacids, hand sanitizer and antihistamine. Bring a pair of travel scissors, nail clipper with nail file. These things are light so there's no good excuse for skipping them. Not full-size containers, just a decent amount in button bags or small containers. A half-used foam tape is smaller and suffices.

Blisters. The trick with blisters is not to put a bandage over it but to build up the area around it so pressure right on the blister is relieved. If changing shoes removes contact, do that. You can, how-ever, wear the same shoes and still make a good day of it, not unaware but not crippled by it, with a few layers of foam tape or regular tape and packing around it, or by cutting a hole in the

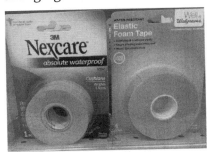

Foam tape.

padded part of a bandaid (or three of them ganged on top of each other).

Try not to pop it. If you feel you need to because it sticks up so much, use one poke of a pin that's been steril-ized with hand sanitizer for at least forty seconds. Never remove the skin, and if it's half off make every effort to lay it back down.

Apply generous globs of Carmex to the blister whether popped or not. Repeat the Carmex application two or three times a day if you can. It keeps it soft and intact. If you remove the skin over a blister, you will be shocked at how much that spot now hurts. Sock or shoe touching that part is not going to be possible without crying. To illustrate how serious I am about this, did you know that soldiers in basic training are given the day off, and then some, if they report a blister whose skin has come off? Drill sergeants are not known for coddling recruits. In any case, Carmex, Carmex, Carmex to shorten the duration of inconvenience from the blister as much as possible.

Ordinary cuts and torn hangnails. The goal is to speed healing and prevent it from opening a second time. If you have an individually packaged hand sanitizer wipe, use it to clean the spot. It will sting. The little wipe can also serve as a wrap until bleeding slows. Don't be too quick to bandage it, because if the bleeding hasn't stopped that bandage may need to be discarded a minute later, and you probably didn't bring that many. As soon as you can get to soap and water, wash it thoroughly, even if you put Carmex on it ten minutes ago. Any kind of soap will work fine.

Washing a cut with soap and water within fifteen minutes or so of occurrence can reduce time-to-heal by two days, so make a champion effort to do this.

Apply hand sanitizer three to five times per day. Restaurants and counters at stores often have a dispenser; if you look around you'll spot them. At gelato (ice cream) stores, ask for a wipe; they usually have them for sticky fingers.

Carmex is applied the same way as an antibiotic cream, about twice a day or between washings.

Pinched finger. A finger that's been pinched, causing blood to pool under the nail is painful. There is a fix for this, but it requires a moment of bravery. You can do it yourself, but the angle and control is better if someone does it for you.

Open up a paper clip to make a wire out of it and heat one end over a flame until it is red hot. Place the hand nearby, then swiftly, while still red, use it to melt a hole into the nail.

It does not require force, just a light push for $1/32^{nd}$ of an inch and then withdraw. The blood will burble out, so have a tissue ready. The reason it doesn't burn the tender tissue under the nail is because the blood is a pool under the nail and the hot thing never goes that deep. Blessed relief. Sometimes it may need to be done again several hours later a little off to the side. As always, apply Carmex and a bandage. The hole grows out, eventually.

If this makes everyone in your party too squeamish, mention it to other travelers; you just may bump into a nurse or a father of eight who has done it several times before.

WoundSeal. This is a powder that will stop bleeding instantly. It works for people on blood thinners because it doesn't depend upon the usual blood clotting factors to work. On any cut or nosebleed, it combines with blood to form a glue that becomes an instant scab over the wound. A four-pack is available at Walgreens and online for about $8; they make a kit with a dispenser for nosebleeds too. No matter what the applicator shape, it's exactly the same ingredient.

Antihistamine. It's very common to react to something on vacation, even if you've never had an allergic reaction before. It's a real timesaver to have a couple of these in a foil sheet and not have to go hunting for a store that sells it. If hives develop, red welts develop on both sides of the body (both arms, both legs, whole torso, and so on), eyes swell or get itchy, stuffy nose, there is itchiness on both sides, speak to a doctor or nurse and if they recommend it, you can take it immediately. The standard brands like Claritin, Benadryl, Allegra or Zyrtec are good choices. Benadryl will cause drowsiness, which may allow it to do double-duty for help sleeping. These may react with other medications, so share that with your medical advisor. Testing the dosage a few days before the trip to gauge side effects is a good idea.

First Aid Kit List
Adhesive bandages

Folding scissors
Ibuprofen
Carmex
Birth control items
Antacid
Medication you need
Antihistamine pills
Anti-diarrheal pills
Hand sanitizer/single packs
Foam tape
Liquid ibuprofen (for children)
Copies of prescription for vital medications

Dirty clothes. A regular plastic bag works fine for stashing dirty clothes. The plastic bags collected from purchases along the way serve for wet swimsuits, bakery I want to bring on the return flight, and dirty clothes. Dirty clothes are the reason to leave excess space in your luggage when heading out. As your precise nesting of items gets disrupted by the segregation of dirty clothes, it gets harder to close the luggage.

Tips on laundering. Launder underwear, bras, or any clothing by wearing them into the shower with you. Yes, it sounds funny and will feel funny. Get them wet, then use shampoo. Rinse. Remove and set aside. For parts you couldn't properly scrub while wearing, once they're off, rub two sides together between your knuckles to attend to the dirty spots. Rinse and set outside the shower until you're done. Wring out. After you're dry, squeeze the clothes in a towel to get most of the moisture out.

If you're showering in the morning, not evening, and leaving this hotel today, then bag the damp clothes and hang them after arrival in your next hotel.

Drying clothes fast: if you hang an item, the part at the bottom will be damp the longest. For tops, damp at the waist will make you miserable for hours, but damp at the collar will dry in about twenty minutes, thanks to body heat.

Use the pants clip on a hanger to hang tops upside down to dry.

Wet clothes seldom dry well in a bathroom. To dry clothes quickly, use one of these methods:

1) using safety pins or binder clips, pin the clothes to the curtain. This works beautifully if the heater/AC is right below the window. Start running it on high, hot or cold; both work.

2) hang wet clothes on paired hangers (allows more space for airflow in the middle) and hang from a floor lamp, wall sconce or other feature so the clothes are not against the wall and air reaches all sides.

3) pin or clip over air vents wherever they are located. Flip clothes every hour or so to expose new areas.

4) lay over the back of an upholstered chair or end of the bed—the water wicks out into the chair/sheet, which becomes wet, but the clothes get drier. Flip or move to a dry spot a few times.

5) drape clothes over a lampshade and turn the lamp on. Watch for too much heat with this, and rotate the clothes.

Laundering in mid-trip. For trips over ten days, finding a regular washing machine to launder everything makes sense.

Wrinkled clothing. Remove wrinkles with a blow dryer. Sprinkle heavy creases with water, or wet your hands and wipe them on the wrinkled clothing for some wrinkle-releasing help. Or ask the front desk for an iron if there isn't one in the closet. Or wear all black. Harder to see the wrinkles.

Extra Stuff: How to Leave it Home

Every day, a person wears a top, bottom, shoes and undergarments. The traveler with four suitcases for a nine day trip doesn't come home with four times more dirty laundry than the one suitcase person. They both come home with roughly the same amount of dirty laundry, but the heavy packer returns home with a lot more clean clothing that can go right back on the hanger. Not dragging around unused items is all it takes.

People who pack heavy simply pack by impression, throwing stuff they might need, clothes they like, or things they use fairly frequently at home into luggage. Then when they are on vacation they're missing stuff they need. So next time they pack even heavier.

People who pack heavy do not have everything they want in their bags. They have four pairs of shoes but not the ones they want to wear with this outfit. They have nine pairs of socks but not the ones that go well with these pants. They bring expensive binoculars along but on the day they go to the Vatican don't bring them because they're so heavy.

Ironically, packing heavy does not mean you are better prepared. Packing heavy means you pretend you don't know yourself, you're really packing for some stranger who might do or encounter anything on this trip. Some stranger who will be mountain climbing, swimming in rivers, waiting for buses on seedy sides of town after dark and attending the Governor's Ball all in the same six-day trip. If that sounds like your trip, then certainly bring that extra daypack, two swimsuits plus beach shoes, the calf-length baggy raincoat and satin dress with matching shoes.

Few hotels in Italian cities have pools, so skip the swimsuit unless the beach is part of your plans. Skip spike heels—most cities have too much uneven terrain. You don't need to skip high heels, just consider a wedge heel.

The packing can't be too precise because you'll have to duplicate it every two or three days. Things can't fit in there 'just so' because as time progresses the clean clothes become dirty and you'll want to segregate them in bags.

Packing up is already going to be a thirty minute job; don't make it take longer.

If all your clean socks and underwear are squirreled away in tiny gaps and stuffed into shoes, how will things fit when the dirty ones are balled up in a bag?

Ignore all advice about scientific, filling-every-gap packing. All undies go into the cloth bag.

On day five it ought to be possible to look at the clock, mutter 'oh my gosh' and simply push things willy-nilly into your luggage in ninety seconds flat and pull that zipper. Worry about wrinkles or even leaking bottles later on. If you can't pull that zipper because you have to fold eight items just so in a bag that you kneel on while you roll it up, you could miss that train, bus, boat or plane.

What to bring

Even if you are checking a bag, there are several items you must pack in carry-on. All your medications, break-ables, jewelry, papers and money go in your carry-on, as well as a few clothing items to last a day if needed. Anything that would be upsetting to lose goes in carry-on.

Food you can bring from home, in your carry-on: Fritos, chips of all sorts, nuts, Pop Tarts, gum, granola, trail mix, cookies, crackers, candy bars, hard candies and bread. You can bring dry packages that need hot water to reconstitute, such as oatmeal and soup. When the beverage cart gets to your row, ask for a cup of hot water. They carry it for hot tea.

Food you can't bring from home, unless it is in a small container in your liquids baggie: liquids, peanut butter, jelly or jar food. Ham salad or other mushy food. Avoid stinky foods like beef jerky, cooked veggies, etc.

Baby and toddler food is allowed; check the TSA website for details.

http://www.tsa.gov/traveler-information/traveling-children

The important thing is, don't hide it or forget to mention it. Present it up front. It's a longer fuss-fuss if they find jars of baby food or formula in your carry-on that you didn't mention. If you decide to bring liquor in a checked bag, bring it in a plastic bottle, not glass. Many liquors are sold in plastic bottles now; if you favorite kind is not, pour it into one that is. Even then, put each one inside a big ziploc bag AND nest it in the middle of all your clothes, not along an edge. Fill it. Half full or less will be subject to air pressure squeezing and puffing, which could create a crack.

What not to bring

Knife. It will get confiscated and it isn't a big help (a travel scissors will get more use)

Matches, liquid fuel or a lighter. These are not allowed in either checked or carry-on. There are special lighters that are allowed in checked but not carry-on, but few people have those. Disposables, never. If you need these, you'll have to pick them up after you arrive. In every airport, that means you'll have to walk possibly fifty steps once you exit the plane to the inevitable store that carries lighters and matches, along with gum and candy bars. Cordless hair curlers use liquid fuel. These used to be called travel curlers, but now they're only appropriate for camping trips, bus or car trips.

Sparkly dress. It will get fallout on everything.

Sewing kit. Do you use it at home? Why would you use it on vacation?

Wash cloth, soap. Unlike hotels farther north, Italian hotels have these.

Pompeii. The one place you should bring your water bottle along. It can be refilled from street fountains. Drinking real Pompeii water, how great is that? Bring your hat too.

110-220V converter. Most of the time. If you read the tiny print on many of today's chargers and accessories, they say they're good for 110-220V or 120-240V, and 50 to 60 Hz. With these, all you need is a plug adapter. Converters will burn out supplying anything that draws more power than a computer brick anyway.

Three things are not allowed in most museums, palaces and churches. Leave these in the hotel room or car.

1. Umbrella. The reasons are sound; in the past umbrellas have been used to reach past fencing and damage priceless art. The foldup ones extend; you aren't fooling anyone because it's short. Tour guides may have them because they work there. Yours is still not OK.

2. Water bottle. When water is thrown on paintings, or even inadvertently splashed, it can cause damage that takes tens of thousands of dollars of restoration to fix. Museums have drinking fountains by the restrooms.

3. Backpack or briefcase-size bag. They can harbor all kinds of heavy items which can be tossed at irreplaceable artworks. Or be used to steal stuff.

Don't imagine you can smuggle yours through. Many attractions in Italy have baggage scanners and metal detectors at the doors. You clog up the line when you bring these items, taking five to ten times longer to process. Little old lady, outside, standing, fainting, hitting head. Your fault.

Seriously, you're in a city; there's no need to schlep around any more stuff than you might take to work. Even a small pile of just-in-case items will take up no more room than a fat wallet.

For spare garments and possible purchases, bring along a string bag. You can wear it like a backpack most of the day, and a string bag is an allowed size and configuration.

On left, a pot in the Museo Archaeologico Nazionale di Napoli, the National Archaeological Museum in Naples. On right, a bit of wall artwork in one of the rooms at Pompeii. The same sort of thing? A ceremonial piece, similar to a wedding cake or anniversary dish? You can't see it here, but the pot has the little notches on the rim portrayed in the wall painting.

Packing List

Add items of relevance to your life and needs. For instance, I bring teabags and creamer, since I don't like powdered creamer. Lately I bring antacid, which I didn't need years ago. I like to travel with a coffee mug, eyeshades, and a magic marker. Other people swear that duct tape and scarves are indispensable.

Travelers will have to flesh out their makeup list themselves.

Everyone will have to add medicines and personal care items they require.

Organize your list by container, not by purpose. That means some clothes could be in the luggage, and others in the 'personal item' carry-on. The most likely reason to forget something is assuming it's in another container.

If one of your containers is 'coat pocket' or 'money belt' then list it, so when you do your touch check you include that location.

Main suitcase, duffel, backpack:

One bottom for every three days

One top per day minus two(eight day trip, six tops); at least one is sweater or warm top

Socks to go with walking shoes (shoes worn on plane, not packed)

underwear

flip-flops (or sandals)

Cloth slippers/hotel fleece socks

sun hat or baseball cap

thin raincoat or waterproof windbreaker

extra tissue packs

Business card with your cell and a US person's phone

individual pack sanitizer wipes, several per person

Ziploc plastic bags, three sizes

String bag (for purchases or serving as a daybag for raincoat storage)

Copy of passport (the page with the photo)

One pair shoes (maximum, omit if sandals will suffice)

Optional: covered plastic thermal coffee mug, sleepwear, swimsuit, swimming cap, polyester (silky) bathrobe/swim coverup, small travel 110/220V blow dryer, Tampons/Maxi-Pads, Birth Control, one fine dining outfit, shawl, small binoculars or opera glasses

Liquids 1 quart bag

Moisturizer

Lipstick or lip balm

Carmex

toothpaste

Sunscreen and bug spray

Optional: nail polish, liquid makeup, hand sanitizer, shaving cream, perfume, after shave, shampoo, conditioner, hair gel, Mio (or equivalent) water flavorer, contact lens care, liquor (in 3.4 oz. bottle or less), nose spray (moisturizer)

Toiletry bag

Powder and other makeup (make a detailed list)

hairbrush

mirror

toothbrush

razor

Ibuprophen and vitamins

Antacid tablets

Antihistamine pills

Travel scissors

safety pins

floss sticks or dental floss

Adhesive bandages

Nail clipper with small file

moleskin, foam tape

Optional: string, duct tape, talcum powder (put in a smaller container), spices, styptic pencil, shower cap, two S-hooks for hanging things

Electronics sack

Second spare phone charger cord

Kitchen timer, 24 hour

Outlet adapter for chargers

USB charger plug for devices

Business card with your cell and a US person's phone

Printed phone number list

Optional: clock for bathroom, multi-outlet extension cord/plug unit rated for 220-240V, camera, camera batteries, camera data storage, waterproof sleeve for phone, bluetooth headset and charger cord. Power converter (only needed if light-draw appliance isn't rated for 220V or 240V)

Carry-on Personal Item

Passport

Driver's license

Phone and phone cord

Euros and Dollars

Credit cards, ATM card

Insurance cards, auto and health

Neck pillow for plane

Aux. portable battery for phone/small electronics

3.5mm stereo headset (earbuds)

Subway pass, parking ticket (airport)

Empty water bottle – fill after scanners

Bottle clip-on, to clip bottle to luggage or belt loop

Flight, car rental, tour and hotel confirmations

maps

eye shades and earplugs

three individual packet sanitizer wipes (minimum)

Sunglasses and spare prescription glasses

two pens

Medicine

Tissue pack

Business card with your cell and a US person's phone

Address list for postcards

USB stick with contacts list, all your websites, emails, documents, scans, photos, etc. from my home computer (can also be extra storage for digital photos), Scan of passport on there.

Breath gum

Optional: Magic marker, small notepad, reading material, book or Kindle, earrings, fiber tablets, face powder, non-liquid makeup

ITALY– THE CHIP BIN TALK

Everyone who goes to Italy will have to leave some wonderful activities and sights for next time. Even if you had months at your disposal, trying to do too much in one trip makes it a muddy mish-mash in your memory, a grueling march you obligated yourself to undertake.

So enjoy whatever you can do or end up doing. Close the door on thoughts about what you missed. Because everyone misses more than they see. The only solution is another trip later on.

~ ~ ~

Years ago I worked for a race car crankshaft manufacturer that made other auto parts as well. I usually gave tours to engineers or auto manufacturer procurement agents, but one day I gave the tour to a high-level, intelligent group comprised mainly of professionals in finance, computers, insurance and business. The tour wove a path through the machine shop, past our huge pin-throw machining lathes, our precision gauges, our high speed CNC milling equipment, and our semi-automated compressed-air-powered fixturing (which I had designed). I was proud to show off this state-of-the-art equipment, some of it costing close to half a million dollars.

But I kept losing my group.

They were stopping to stare at something they found enthralling: the chip bins. These are the waist-high, 4 x 7 foot metal tubs where we dump the scrap metal cut off during machining.

Perceiving that staring at the splash guards of humming grinders that were holding .0001" tolerances this very second could never compete with the rich variety in the chip bins, I abandoned my planned machine shop talk and explained how the various chips are made, why some are fat and blue while others are lacy coils of silver or radiant gold (aluminum and copper, respectively). I told them what the color and the curl of the chip tells us about the metal composition, the type of machine that made it, and the machine feed and speed. I picked up two chips from the same machine to show how the color and the ragged edges tell us when the tool is getting dull and needs changing. My audience pointed to one chip after another and asked "What about this one?" At the end, I fetched some baggies and let them all pick a few chips to take home with them. They enjoyed themselves and said they learned a lot. I guess they did. It just wasn't the way a pro wants to come at it.

This chapter is the chip-bin talk about Italy and overseas travel.

It won't really be like other travel guides, just like I didn't really give a machine shop tour. What experienced people want you to know and firmly believe is the important stuff isn't what a newbie can use to make any sense of it.

Sleeping while on vacation. Most people find they wake up more in the night when sleeping in a strange bed in a strange place. It might seem like this less-perfect sleep is detrimental. Good news! It's not so bad. Scientists studying sleep found that the value of sleep, the bit that makes us feel well-rested, is the REM sleep. It occurs in a cycle that starts as we fall asleep. Waking up more often resets the clock, so to speak, so we actually get more REM sleep in less time if we wake up a few times in the night. This is why a ninety minute nap in the afternoon is equivalent to more than three hours of sleep in the night.

Getting repeatedly awakened by noises or lights will leave us cranky the next day, but merely not sleeping 'as good' as we do at home isn't something to worry about. Before you start believing sleep is an issue, think about whether you napped on the train or dozed a bit while sitting on a bench today. Those count. You might be waking up at 5 AM just because now you have enough sleep.

White noise. Some people travel with a white noise maker, finding it covers those new-to-me noises and hallway voices that our brain instinctively strains to comprehend, thereby disrupting the inattention necessary to fall asleep. There are white noise apps on phones too. A bathroom fan left on may provide a nice white noise. Try the white noise generator for several nights at home to see which works best for you—waves on the beach, wind through the trees, soft classical music or fifty other choices. Covering up those tiny strange-room noises may be all you need to sleep well.

Coffee. Italy has a love affair with coffee. Getting sufficient great coffee will never be a problem. Their custom is to drink latte only in the morning, but they're used to tourists. Many hotels offer free coffee from a machine—I think they all have the exact same cappuccino machine. The cups are small but you can go for thirds or fourths. You will get quite the buzz if you do. Italians don't do that; they drink one at a time, but two hours later are getting another, while Americans are still running on the spurt from their mega cups.

Another custom here is to drink the morning coffee with bakery while standing up. If you step into a place where half the people are standing and eating even with chairs available, nothing is wrong with those chairs, you've just entered an establishment catering to locals.

Paying for food and transportation. You will find many procedures in Italy seem to depend upon the honor system to the casual onlooker. This could entail finding the pay station in a restaurant yourself, or struggling to the front of a bus to validate a bus ticket, or not getting on public transportation until the pass is authorized. Do not be fooled. They have far sharper eyes for scofflaws than you are accustomed to in the states, and the fines and punishments will seem over the top to you. Whether it's stepping out of a restaurant without paying or using public transportation without getting your ticket date-stamped, getting caught is going to ruin your day. Assume that they have their antenna up about tourists. If you make your cheaty move and then try to play dumb if caught, it won't fly. No one from the US can say 'where I come from, food and transportation are free.' Pay the people, and if you can't tell how to do that, ask. Don't leave the area until you're sure you have paid.

Hotel bathrooms. Avert misery by closing the sink stopper or laying a hand towel flat over it before putting in contacts, taking a ring off, putting on earrings or taking a pill anywhere in the sink area. This is unfamiliar territory; things can take a bad bounce. If it's smaller than your entire index finger, cover the drain. Close the toilet lid for the same reason.

Toilets in Italy have a far wider range of appearances than those in the US. Some have wooden seats, others just have the porcelain. Some seem way too low for our liking. You can 'hover' over it or actually park thighs on the cold porcelain. I suggest doing some very slow knee bends twice a day for a week or two before heading out, to build up some tolerance for a fifty second 'hover.'

Few toilets are comfortable enough to want to sit there longer than it takes to do business. I'm pretty certain there's no reading on the throne like the US, where actual books are written just for throne-reading.

Press circle in the wall box to flush the toilet. When using the bidet, run the water until the warm water arrives.

Step on the silver box on the floor: step on it to flush the toilet; how neat is that?

VAT Tax

When you purchase a big ticket item in Italy, there is a thing called the VAT tax. It's rather steep, 22% in 2013, but as an American tourist you don't have to pay it.

I bought a pair of gold earrings in Florence and met the monster. Here's my story.

In shops, the sales rep will talk you out of paying the VAT tax in the store. In lieu of paying the tax, they hand you a voucher that he or she says is easy to get stamped in the airport and then drop in a mailbox. She will probably tell you the passport-checking guy will stamp it. That's a lie. They're mistaken. Not only isn't it a 'stamp,' but there is only one specific container the completed form can be placed in at the airport, not a mailbox.

I can't speak for the other airports, but at the Rome Fiumicino airport, they do not stamp it at the passport checkers. There is a single location in Gate H for the duty-free counters. It is a tram ride distant from Gate G, plus up and down steps, say about twenty minutes at a good clip. Three of the four booths have short lines and the fourth has a huge line. The huge line is for the 'simple stamp.'

In the shoulder season of May, which is about 30% as busy as it's going to be in July, the line for that 'stamp' was a long winding snake that budged by about one customer every ten minutes. I had two hours before my flight and after thirty minutes in line it was apparent I would either miss my flight or save the VAT tax. Since the store reports the sale with your credit card number, when you don't supply your properly authorized form within X amount of days, they ding your credit card for the VAT a few months later. You and I know that the store report contains everything they need to absolve you from VAT tax; the airport thing is simply a wrench in the works to make you pay it anyway.

Even if you get the form approved in the airport, if you don't place it into the specific container, your credit card will be dinged for the VAT tax anyway. If the line is too long, dropping the fully complete but non-validated form in the correct container or buying overseas stamps and mailing it once you get home means the VAT tax will show up on your card a few months later.

Why doesn't the airport VAT tax counter simply have the 'specific container' beside their desks? Well, that would eliminate an element of tourist error that adds hundreds of thousands of euros to their coffers. The one-and-only specific container is poorly marked and *not within sight* of the booth where you get the paperwork approved. It's about one hundred feet away. You must *walk past a bank of regular mailboxes* to get to it. As we all know, if you drop a letter without postage into a mailbox, the letter is discarded. Sneaky devils, they want you to accidentally do that.

On the other hand, for those who PAID the VAT tax in the store at purchase time and merely need a refund, the line was five people long on the afternoon I was there. Those people were served in about three minutes each. I went to that line and asked if they had a stamp for this form, and they said no. They laughed at me, because it turns out it's not a rubber stamp at all. It's something akin to a credit check. The Refund line had three windows with two customers each, but they could not help out with the five-hour long line thirty feet away. They sat around chatting with each other.

No one arrives seven hours early to the airport to wait out the VAT tax line, so Italy gets the VAT tax for certain. My hunch is that vendors are given an incentive for pushing the 'simple stamp' option because Italy knows exactly what it's doing.

Think for yourself, but when I go back to Italy, not on your life will I chose the option of skipping the VAT tax in the store. I'll pay it at purchase, then at the Rome airport, stand in the dinky and quick line for the refund.

I doubt procedures will change, being so lucrative for Italy. Unless you find something dated after March 2014 that contains real proof that the Rome airport added about ten windows to the no-VAT booth or have ceased to require airport 'simple stamp', this is how it is.

Understanding Italian Restaurants

The following is the truth, so help me: look it up elsewhere if you don't believe it.

Wine: The house wines are usually pretty good. A restaurant may have a red or white wine choice. Unlike in the US where the house wine can be rotgut no-name swill (make it tolerable by mixing it with any soda or even just add water), the house wine in Italy is their signature. They give it a lot of thought, and the locals even prefer a restaurant because of the wine. Sometimes they cut deals with actual grape farmers (wineries) to get a lock on their signature wine. Just like restaurant connoisseurs tell you to take the daily special because the cook is putting extra love into that dish today, give the house wine a try because Italian restaurants hinge their reputations on it.

Tipping: Restaurant staff are paid a decent wage in Italy. Tipping is uncommon. You might tip if you asked the waiter to make a local phone call for you or he helped you link to the restaurant's Wi-Fi, but they do not expect tips and probably fewer than 10% of the local customers tip.

Time and again, Americans will write a review like this: "The service was great, the waiter was attentive, and then after the last drink refill he disappeared. We waited forty-five minutes for the check, then had to get up and go find him. He didn't have anything written down, asked ME what we ordered, unbelievably unprofessional. We were so mad we didn't tip." Ha-ha-ha-ha! Not only was he providing perfect Italian service, he was most likely unaware that he was being slighted by no tip.

Most of the restaurant protocols in the US and Italy are identical until near the end. Italian culture says it's rude to give good customers the bum's rush as soon as they clean their plates. Restaurants are there to provide food, but also to provide respite from crowded, noisy homes and demanding relatives, as well as provide a place for business wheeling and dealing. The myth is that dining companions may become so engrossed in their conversation they lose track of time. No Italian restaurant condones intruding upon after-dinner conversation simply for the financial gain of clearing the table for the next customer. You could sit there all day, waiting for that check.

Now, you'd think that wouldn't apply to the solo diner who is simply reading facebook posts, but you'd be wrong. Perhaps the thinking goes . . . this traveler found this oasis of Wi-Fi and is getting valuable updates on the health of his parents, so to give him the bum's rush before he gets to today's update is heartless or cruel. Or similar people-oriented theory. An Italian server will never interrupt your solitaire game or facebook scrolling by offering you a check. You could sit there all day, waiting.

This is the concept behind restaurants in Italy: The restaurant loves you, wishes you to stay, hates to see you leave, must you really go, oh you want to talk about money, ugh, well I guess we have to, but only if you insist.

Does he know what you ordered? You betcha. He brought the food, didn't he? People who exercise their mind to log lists of items into short term memory find that it comes easier than you imagine. Actors memorize two hours of Shakespearian dialog in a couple of weeks. Not all actors are of physicist caliber. A waiter or waitress can remember twenty seconds worth of items, no problem. We humans have a built-in ability to memorize like this. It goes dormant with disuse, but we all have it.

When your Italian waiter or waitress acts a little unclear on what you ordered, they are just being polite. Don't be fooled; they know exactly what you had. The idea is that they encourage you to provide half the list, and they'll provide half the list. Don't even think of saying you ordered the €8 carbonera instead of the €12 shrimp pasta.

Here's what you do:

Eat, drink, and when you're done and ready to go, simply stand up. Step to the side and scoot your chair under the table. Your whole party does the same. Slowly, calmly collect your belongings. Nine times out of ten your server will appear from nowhere. If he has not yet appeared, scan the horizon and make eye contact with any employee. Smile, nod or just look blank, whatever you wish. Do not talk. Server appears. The two of you will review what you ordered, and he will write it down in front of you. Give him your credit card. When you sign, you can review the charges to your comfort level, pay and leave.

You can sit and ask for the check as your waiter or waitress goes by, but that will usually take a few minutes longer since they must lend the impression that the restaurant is in no hurry for you to leave, they like you and enjoy your company. If you don't mind that, it's fine.

In some restaurants there is a podium where people pay their bills. Our custom in the US is the server leaves the check on the table, face down (our little nod to not looking so profiteering), so when we're ready to go we take it to the podium. In Italy, you simply walk to the podium and your server will appear. Or the person at the podium will know who your server is by where you were sitting and get their attention.

Either way, it's actually faster and more attentive than the US system.

It's possible some restaurants coach their staff in American protocols. All it does is make you even more certain you're getting bad service at Italian-protocol restaurants.

If you step back and think about it, when dining in the US, have you ever distinctly felt the restaurant was rushing you? Just wanted your table for the next customer? Have you ever grown tired of waiting for the server to bring the check? Were you ever annoyed because something you ordered but never got is on the bill? Well that doesn't happen in Italy. Enjoy.

Tourist Cards

All the major cities have tourist cards. I could write paragraphs on each and next year they could change them, so I'll only point you to the websites so you can check this year's prices, included museums, and included transportation.

Some provide free admission to listed locales, while others may have the first two free and the rest at a discount, and others just a discount on all. Some include free entry on the local public transportation, while others give a significant discount on the fare. For some, the card itself is your bus or train pass, while others require you to stand in line to get the ticket or validate the pass.

They can be purchased at the train station by the amount of days and the scope of the benefits. The website has a list of locations where they are sold.

They are a good idea for the sight-seeing traveler, even with all the conflicting information you might read. Most of the confusion is caused by old information; check the date on every tourist card comment you read; when they are older than eighteen months, be cautious about trusting it.

The websites themselves are cagey about telling you what the actual discount is by event, and abound with marketing extravagance. Basically, if you're going to do a few of the top attractions in that town, want to be spontaneous but hate standing in line, the cards are perfect for you: you'll break even or end up a few bucks ahead.

Every person needs their own card.

Popular attractions.

The cards can't do magic; they can't get you into venues that are sold out. Some attractions sell out weeks ahead. Go online to buy tickets as early as possible. These include the

Vatican or the Galleria dell' Accademia in Florence, where the David statue resides, to name two. I can't list all the places that might be sold out on the day you show up at the door. If it's important to you, go online and pay in full before leaving home. Regret is a bitch.

Lean toward getting the tourist card.

Don't feel cheap for doing this. These cards are a huge marketing thing for the venues, and the more people who use it, the more brownie points/percentage that venue gets. They treat you better with the card because they're ranked by card usage. Look at it this way: the card price is the real price, the walk-up price is a penalty, a punishment for not doing it the right way.

Online, glance through the long list of places and things that take the card, but don't try to memorize them, just absorb by osmosis or use for ideas. When you're there, pull it out whenever you're going to spend money and ask. They will either shake their heads no, or say yes. No harm, no foul.

When in doubt, whip it out.

The cards have either a magnetic (black) strip or an RFID chip. This is basically a so-what, except: magnetic strips can be wiped by anything with a speaker in it, like the clock radio. Speakers have magnets, and the bigger the speaker, the bigger the magnet. As you may have noticed, magnets have a real short range. Two inches is a mile with them. Souvenir refrigerator magnets placed in the same pocket with the tourist card can be a big mistake. Putting both into the same purse, just on different sides, is fine.

The best reason to buy the tourist card is that attractions have a separate line for cardholders and tour groups that is always much shorter, so you spend less time in line. During peak times this is hours! But even in the slow season this reduces standing in line by thirty minutes. Without shade. In the rain. The value of the card is measured in time, not money.

The cards often reduce the cost of the audio tour, too.

A last word about these cards. They're a first choice for those spending two to five days in Rome, Florence, Venice, Milan or Naples. They work so well because not one out of twenty gets them. Their breeze-through line would be huge too if all the tourists bought them. When you have the card, you feel like a genius.

Exceptions, when you can skip the card:

When you book tour guides ahead of time whose price includes the tickets. Note, some online tours do not provide the ticket! Always read carefully; it is often tiny print that says ticket not included—then your tourist card is handy.

If you won't use the local transportation or have a car (driving is not the best way to get around Rome, Naples, Florence, and is not even an option in Venice), then half their value goes away.

You're taking in only one or two tourist attractions and think standing in line is part of the fun.

You bought your tickets before you left home. If they weren't mailed to you, you'll pick them up at shorter-line windows at the venue.

Rome: RomaPass
http://www.romapass.it

Good for three days. Can be purchased at all participating museums, at the airport, and at the Termini train station plus a few other subway and train stations.

Free use of city buses and subways around Rome. Does not include transportation to and from the airport.

Free entry into the first two places you use the pass. Most people go to the two most expensive places first. The Colosseum/Roman Forum is a good pick. If you go to a much cheaper venue first and don't want to blow your freebies there, simply don't show the card and pay like normal. After the free events, there is a discount for all other sites, and the shorter line is yours. There is a good free map.

Does not include the Vatican.

The Pantheon is free, always.

At the Colosseum, passholders have their own turnstile to breeze right in. The lines at the Colosseum can be brutal, so it's worth it just for this.

Roma and Piu Pass

http://www.romapass.it

An extended pass that includes the more far-flung archeological sites. It also includes Zone A and B, a wider zone of public transportation, but again, not the airport.

Rome Tours

If you Google **Rome Tour**, there are hundreds, most with sterling reviews. Not to detract from the enjoyment they provide, but almost every site can be well served with the audio tour or using the collect-a-group guides on site. It's a matter of time and best use of your resources. If you read a lot of archeology stuff (my first major was archeology) or even read about it on Wikipedia before you go, a guide will not tell you much that is new. But they might have an intriguing spin on the facts plus insert some never-fail humorous asides. The good ones will point out a few interesting spots you may not have found yourself, and will follow an efficient route, not the snakey, oops wrong way route you'll take. This is actually true everywhere, not just Rome.

Segways have arrived in Rome. Having walked Rome, this tour holds some appeal. I didn't check out the routes, and there might be a minimum amount of people to engage them. I didn't see any of these last year.

http://www.segwayrome.it./

The website says it will throw in a free 110 open ticket and free hotel pickup for advance booking. No price is listed; you have to call.

Florence: Firenze Card

http://www.firenzecard.it

The best card ever

Good for three days

Public transportation, bus and tram, is free

Includes free Wi-Fi areas

Unlike the others, free admission to all the museums on the list for the time duration—and there's a ton of them

You can use the pass line, not the regular line, saving hours

Free admission to the special exhibits too

In peak season a venue could be sold out; book ahead online if it's important to you

Unfortunate plague: Locks on bridges. Lovers ostensibly seal their love by making vows as they secure a lock and throw away the key. Awwww. The downside is it is damaging ancient grillwork, and workers have to cut them off to reduce bridge damage. Rumor has it the custom was invented by a locksmith near Ponte Vecchio to beef up sales.

Venice: Venice Card

http://www.hellovenezia.com/index.php?option=com_content&view=article&id=71&Itemid=130&lang=en

Sorry for the long link, but if you simply enter hellovenezia.com, it takes you to an Italian language version. Of course, that could have been fixed yesterday.

This one gets you discounts at some restaurants too. Buy it at the train station. It's good for seven days. It does not include any transportation, but gets you into the short line and a discount at all tourist attractions.

It used to be at the veniceconnected.com website, which is still active as of this writing, but when you click the "Buy Now" button, it takes you to hellovenezia.

The website has instructions about using the card for public toilet uses.

Vaporetto all-you-can-ride passes, ACTV:
http://goitaly.about.com/od/transportation/qt/vaporetto.htm
The official site is updated frequently, boldly gives all the prices, plus contains many other nifty links for Venice.
www.veniceconnected.com/buy/calendar

This link (hopefully still) takes you to the site in the picture, where you can buy the ACTV cards before you leave the US. They can also be purchased in Venice at the train station, but the lines will be long. If you buy it ahead of time, there are automated machines where you enter the PNR booking code they sent you, and out it pops. The site reminds you that if you buy multiple tickets online, the clock starts ticking on all of them as soon as the first one is validated. If you're buying for two parties whose stays won't begin on the same day, buy them in two batches.

It's worth pointing out that the seven-day pass costs just two rides more than a three-day pass. Saving money by buying a three-day could put your morning return-to-the-train-station trip just outside the pale—and that's the trip with your heavy luggage that you really don't want to walk.

The pass includes going to the island of Murano.

Most stops are one-way; this means to go back to where you came from, you won't go to the stop you were dropped off. It may be a stop on the other side of the canal but nearby, possibly out of sight. A map is the only way you'll know which way to walk.

You can buy a public toilet pass at the same time, and those will be added to your ACTV ticket so you only have one card to carry around. I don't know if they will really check ID to be sure the toilet user is the person who bought the ticket, but they're allowed to ask for ID to use the toilet.

Naples: ArteCard

http://www.campaniartecard.it

Buy it at the Campania-artecard information point at Garibaldi, aka Stazione Di Napoli, the main train station, or right at the museums.

It includes free Unicocampania public transportation—which is only part of the local public transportation, but includes the public buses and subway. The tutta la regione is the one that includes free transportation to Pompeii and Herculaneum.

First two venues are free; the rest are at a discount.

If you are going to these two digs, be warned that they are not clearly marked. You want the **Pompeii Scavi-Villa dei Misteri,** not the town. The Herculaneum site is train stop **Ercolano.** Once you get off the train for Herculaneum you have only an arrow in a direction but it is down their main street so it's hard to get lost. If you walk that way for a few blocks you can't miss it; the way back is a little more iffy, but during tourist season people are going back and forth constantly so if you hang with the tourists or go where they're coming from, you'll muddle through just fine.

Bring a water bottle and a sun hat. The water bottle can be refilled at one of the many water fountains right on the grounds. Both have audio tours that are well worth it because not much signage is written in English.

It's possible and not rushed to do both Pompeii and Herculaneum in the same day if you hop on the train before 9 AM. I intended to eat lunch in a sit-down restaurant in Ercolano, but since visiting these sites was a lifelong dream of mine, I spent too much time at Pompeii so ate in their café on the grounds. A ton of bad reviews may have lowered my standards, but the sandwiches and desserts were perfectly tasty. I'm not a food snob; if the tomato tastes like tomato, the ham tastes like ham, and the almond paste tastes like almonds, I have no complaints. Not to belabor the point, but if you expect butter or mayo on bread in Italy, you will be disappointed. Sandwiches are drier than we like because it is not the US and they make them differently.

Milan: MilanoCard

http://www.milanocard.it/

Available in 24 hour or three-day versions

All public transportation is free for 24 or 48 hours

Three Museums are free, the rest are discounted

Encompasses discounts for tours, restaurants, hotels, stores, airport bus, and more

One Under-ten child card is free with every adult purchase

Bologna: Bologna Welcome Card

http://www.bolognawelcome.com/en/richiedicard/

48 hours, museums plus 24 hours free public transportation

Free admission to several palaces and museums

Discounts at restaurants, shops, theaters, etc.

Audio Tours

Your tourist card often gets you a discount on these, so be sure to show it when buying an audio tour at museums and ancient sites.

Buying the audio tour is a great way to get the most out of your visit. Guided tours are nice, yes better, but they entail planning one's whole day around it. A day with two or even three guided tours scheduled will make you appreciate how annoying hurry-up-and-wait can be.

In Italian museums, the placards beside artworks and antiquities are often in Italian only. Even if it's not your habit to get the audio tour, the next three hours will be much less frustrating if you spring for an English audio set.

The best bang for your buck on person-guided tours is on city tours that explore a neighborhood, such as Rome by Night, Colosseum by Night, or Underground Naples. The Vatican guided tours are also valuable. I had a wonderful guided tour of Venice that culminated in a stop by an sixteenth century archway, the only remnant of Marco Polo's original house. Almost everything on that Venice tour I would not have found or understood on my own.

Audio tour means an audio-only unit. Some of the best ones are Bluetooth activated (my guess) so when you walk near the display it starts telling you about it. For others, you type in the number listed on a placard to begin the story. The worst ones assume a normal pace and you must progress on its timetable. If you want to linger you can pause it, then resume when you're ready.

Video tours have much the same information as the audio tour but are on an iTouch or other device that is able to show you movie clips, reenactments, or maps with moving features. I'm a techy person so if the video unit is only a buck or two more than the audio, I'll take the video. Both are good, but I hope the video tour isn't SO-O good that you walk through the attraction staring at a little screen instead of looking up.

The players come with disposable earbuds. You may prefer to use your own earbuds, which I usually did.

You might have the idea of sharing the audio tour by plugging your two-earphone unit into the jack and huddling close the whole time. Most of the time the audio tour is on just one channel, left or right. Or it might make itself interesting by bopping the sound fully left or fully right, as if two people are talking, but if each of you has one earpiece you get only half the story.

The venue may ask for your passport or driver's license to hold hostage until you return the player. If this is scary to you, consider bringing along an expired driver's license for this purpose. I don't think they really check it, and with all the different US licenses they can't tell.

Only once did I hand over the passport, after that I handed over my driver's license. They were good stewards of my valuables, but they're just clerks, don't really see anything serious going on, and I can envision if the passport were gone when I returned, there is no recourse at all.

If your passport ever disappears, find the nearest US Consulate or office, where they will issue a temporary copy that serves the purpose. The police can help you locate this office if the hotel doesn't know. It doesn't have to be done this minute if you will be in Italy a few more days. It's easier if you have a photocopy or even the passport number written down somewhere. Even if you don't, they make phone calls and so on until they identify you.

Hop-On-Hop-Off (HOHO) buses

I am a huge fan of HOHO buses; they are my #1 choice for first day in a new city. If you just up and leave to a place you've never been before, not a moment of reading up, then find the HOHO. By the end, you'll know how you want to spend your day, and can get off the second time it goes around.

There are great HOHOs in Washington DC, San Francisco, London (I think they invented it), New York, Boston, and I'm sure many others.

In every country, what you can expect is:

A recording, a second person, or the driver has a headset and tells you brief information about the main attractions.

A bumpy ride with a lot of leaning turns.

No seat belts.

On occasion you're encouraged to shout or wave at the locals (to annoy them) or make noise at people not 'as lucky' as you (say, standing in the rain). All in good fun.

A laugh or two. Sometimes it gets carried away and they try too hard to amuse you.

Periods of silence.

You get back on in exactly the same place you were dropped off. This is seldom true with all other modes of street transportation.

HOHOs are plagued by reviews from people who expect too much. It's easy to find fifty reviews that ding the Rome HOHO for hanging on the fringe of the old town. Really? They're holding it against a BUS COMPANY that 800 year old streets are narrow? Are they supposed to finance making streets wider? Ditto with the road being bumpy, bad smells, crowds, too many stoplights, being stuck in traffic. Is the bus company really supposed to get their act together regarding those so the experience is nicer? For crying out loud. I would hold them responsible for scratchy speakers, unintelligible dialog, and dirty windows. But outside the bus, that's the city, folks.

Rome HOHO buses

http://www.trambusopen.com/en/home.cfm

There are several; the one calling itself 110 open is the most common. They are double-decker buses with the top open. They do a loop but can't get that close to some of the main sites; they'll drop you off a few blocks away. You get to see Rome. The Archeobus is another route that goes down the Appian way to some old archeological sites, catacombs, and palaces.

The signage for this bus at Termini is confusing, and called something not written or used anywhere else. If you speak Italian I suppose it's easier to figure out. Ask anyone who works there; they'll point you to the right place. Ask for centodieci; that's 110 in Italian.

http://www.viator.com/tours/Rome/Rome-Hop-On-Hop-Off-Sightseeing-Tour/d511-2916ROME

The Viator buses are garishly red, with blue and yellow to make them pop. You sure know when your bus is coming.

Subways and Trains

Rome Metro – the subway. Direction is indicated by the final stop going in that direction. Laurentina is the south-east end of the blue line, Rebibbia is the north-west end.

Fares

Each city is different, so even if you're a lifelong public transportation rider you'll need to learn the rules. Some systems have ticket or pass options not available from the vending machine banks along the wall. They can only be purchased online or from a person. Vending machines may take 'only' credit cards or 'only' cash. Even their own website will not tell you how to get a ticket or use it, only the price.

Rome subway tickets are good for seventy-five minutes from purchase but for only one ride. Boston tickets, on the other hand, are good for there and back if it's within two hours. In Portland, OR and Naples, Italy buying the ticket and validating it are two different acts at two different machines, but in Naples the fines are horrendous if you don't validate.

In London, the lowest-cost pass is good for an entire day. In some cities a pass will work on the subway, bus and light rail; in others there are separate tickets and price structures for different modes of transportation. In most cities, including Rome, tickets are sold by zone, not distance, so a two-mile trip that crosses two zones costs more than a five-mile trip within a zone. Zones will be a bullseye around the center of a city.

To make it more fun, some routes cost more in one direction than the other. Charging the pass with more money than you think you need is the safe way to handle unexpected exit fees and zone fees, which they collect by requiring carding through turnstyles again upon leaving. If they're thoughtful they'll place at least one working vending machine to load more value onto the card on your side of the exit turnstyle; in communities that don't get many tourists they'll assume you know about the exit charge so there will be literally no mention of it anywhere until that moment. Plus no way to charge a depleted card.

Tourists will usually travel within one zone, but pay attention, because fines can be horrendous for trying to sneak through two zones. As a tourist, you may be oblivious and not trying to pull a fast one, but the authorities long ago ceased to care about making exceptions for tourists, especially when tourists are defined as "people with enough money to come here and with no chance of being related to someone I know."

Don't even think about jumping turnstyles, doubling up, or other money-saving endeavors; they have smart-cams in the ceilings, infrared sensors and footpads that sense this and the police will be on top of you before you reach the platform. Assume this is true in this station and save yourself some grief. You aren't from around here, and that makes it very easy for them to throw the book at you.

Using Public Transportation.

Safety-wise, buses and subways are even-steven. Accidents can happen. Both, however, are safer than driving a rental car in a strange city.

Subway or light rail passengers may have to take stairs to a room with vending machines along one wall. There may be a booth with a person in it. Tickets for one ride or several rides can be purchased there. Your city pass may need to be validated once, after which it works like a bus pass for the duration. Most locals buy a monthly pass or stock up on tickets, which is why they walk without pause. The far end of the room has a waist-high barrier with openings big enough for a person to walk through, the turnstyle. This is the only place one pays for a ride; once past the turnstyles one can hop on when the train arrives.

Google **Rome metro map** or **Naples metro** or **Florence metro**, you get the idea, for any city you are going to visit to get a map of the public transportation system.

Each train line is designated by a color; red, blue, green, yellow and orange are usual. The color is usually painted on the cars prominently, but not always. Sometimes all cars are the same and the color is a small patch on the signs or a placard in the front window. Color matters most in hub stations where several of the colors may arrive on the same track, splitting off to their direction after people have boarded. Most stations have just one color heading in two directions.

When the station is on one side of the tracks, the way to get to the other side is to go up and over, or down and under to get to the other side. Sometimes the doors to either direction split right after the turnstyles and sometimes that split happens only when the tracks are in sight. Have eyeballs all over right from the moment you enter the subway looking for signage. There may be only one sign, and sometimes it is located right by the entry, when your sunlight-adjusted eyes cannot discern the black sign on dark green walls.

There are still tickets in Italy where someone punches a hole into them to indicate they're used. Others have a black strip on one side or both, and this is fed into a slot. The machine will grab this ticket away from you and then return it to you, either out another slot on the far side or the same slot you put it in. This slot will be on the **right side** of a turnstyle or opening gate. Lefties out there, if you feed or hold it to the one on the left side, the fellow next to you gets a free ride and you get nothing.

The other kind feels like a plastic credit card. This kind is often not slid into a slot but held somewhat flat on an area of the turnstyle that usually has a rectangle with a circle or oval embossed on it.

With both types, proceed through the flaps when they open or go through the turnstyle smoothly, without hesitation. These either provide a very short time or are done when motion stops. You could get stuck or have to pay another fare if you don't move forward in a workmanlike fashion. Watch how the other people do it and imitate it.

If the ticket or pass isn't read or checked before boarding or in the car, it may be required to leave the station, so don't discard it in the nearest garbage can upon exiting.

Seating: Statistically the cars at the beginning or end are less full; during busy times that doesn't mean you'll score a seat, but it could make the difference between squeezing on or waiting for the next one. Staying with crowds is safer; off-peak, pick a car with ten or fifteen people, not two.

If you are not a city person, riding in a crowded subway or bus is going to be disconcerting. Yes, people you don't know will be touching you torso to torso. Each rock and stop of the train will cause contact. City people have learned to simply not count this touching as anything. It's fine to say 'excuse me' if the jostle was particularly rough, but everyone understands you're doing your best.

The social contract regarding crowded trips is no touching with hands, and no non-ride-induced pressure.

You can find information on renting a car in Naples or Rome, but think hard about having that be the number one choice. The streets are terribly narrow, and when they're not narrow then restaurants put tables in the streets and vendors set up racks with clothes and purses, plus the motorcycles predict a car's movement and slip through by inches, so if you lose nerve and brake briefly you will wipe those guys out, getting yourself embroiled in a car-scooter accident situation.

Rental car. If you see anything not pristine on the car when you take possession, snap a photo with your phone and discuss it, even just one sentence, with the rental agency employee. If there is any dispute that you caused the damage later, your date and time stamped photos will come in handy.

Italiarail

There are a couple of train companies that run between cities from the same train stations. One can buy either passes or tickets for individual legs.

The passes are a good deal for people spending a long time in Europe or really moving around. Most of us will stay in a city two to four days, so the benefit of a pass doesn't pan out. To make it more complicated, even with a pass some of the trains have reserved seats, so you still have to pick a specific train number and be there on time. Of course if there are seats available they will assign it to you in the train station, but during the busy season that's a big if.

You can google **Italy train travel**, or here are some sites that have good information on trains between cities:

http://www.ricksteves.com/rail/italy.cfm

http://www.italiarail.com/

http://www.tripadvisor.com/Travel-g187768-c19328/Italy:Italy.Train.Travel.html

TRENO will indicate the train number.

CARROZZA is the car number

POSTO is the seat number.

On the Departure board, the track number is listed as BIN or Binario.

POLFER indicates the Italian Police whose duty is on the railways.

While employees going on strike are common in Italy, by law the trains have to announce them two weeks in advance and they cannot last more than twenty-four hours.

Train cars will have a 1 or 2 on the outside, indicating first or second class. At some stations first class will be nearest the station, at others farthest away. At each stop the train pulls out the same way it came in, so the tail becomes the nose.

First class cars have two seats on one side and a solo seat on the other. Most seats face each other with a table between.

Second class cars have two on each side, no tables.

There is overhead storage for luggage. There is also rack storage on one end of the car, but unless you're sitting within eyeshot of those racks, it's better to keep your luggage nearby.

On the train: don't be afraid to improve your lie. In golf terms, I mean if you get on the train and don't like your seat because the window is obstructed or facing backwards (this changes from stop to stop) then move to an empty one. When the conductor comes around to check your ticket, he won't care as long as you're in the same class. (first or second class). Of course if at the next stop someone says that's their seat, you have to go back to your baddie seat. In one case the woman said don't get up, I'll sit in your seat. Well, I mean more or less because she spoke in Italian and I speak only English. But I got her drift, I showed her my ticket, and off she went to sit in my bad-view seat. Napping on train rides is a tradition, and that's what she intended to do so it didn't matter to her.

Actually I fibbed a little there; I had four years of high school Spanish many moons ago, so I can muddle through making out spoken or written Italian. When I speak I universally annoy them with my wrong choice of vowel, but I can communicate a bit.

I improved my lie on three separate train trips, braced myself to answer questions, and the conductor didn't bother. I suppose his logic is, I ask, the passenger comes up with a reason, and then I allow it. So he cuts to the chase: if no one is complaining, nothing is wrong.

If you buy online, you get a seat assignment right away. If you're traveling with a rail pass, you need to get a seat sometime before you board, the earlier the better. I found buying the Trenitalia tickets online to be easy, highly visible on all the choices, and efficient. If you buy a few months ahead of time you can purchase first class tickets for less than the cost of second class the day of the trip.

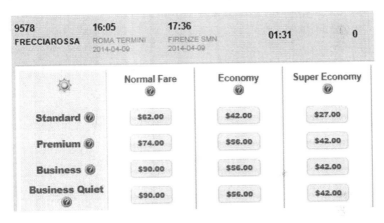

| 9578 FRECCIAROSSA | 16:05 ROMA TERMINI 2014-04-09 | 17:36 FIRENZE SMN 2014-04-09 | 01:31 | 0 |

☼	Normal Fare ✓	Economy ✓	Super Economy ✓
Standard ✓	$62.00	$42.00	$27.00
Premium ✓	$74.00	$56.00	$42.00
Business ✓	$90.00	$56.00	$42.00
Business Quiet ✓	$90.00	$56.00	$42.00

There are several prices posted online. There is no difference in the seats; the only difference materializes if you miss the train, not if you ride it.

Should you worry? If you buy the super economy first class train ticket from Rome to Florence three months ahead, for example, you would be out $42 if you missed it. Is that worth paying $90 so you can get your money back on the 5% chance you miss the train? Not in my book.

If you have other trip insurance through your credit card or your homeowner's insurance, you may be covered for the $42 if you plans are cancelled for an allowed reason.

Sightseeing from the train: My plan was to see a bit of Tuscany while traveling between Rome and Florence. I caught only glimpses. The train goes through frequent and long pitch black tunnels. The route is straight because the train goes under the hills instead of looping around.

First class: do it for the seats, not the free refreshments. Don't count on that soft drink and snack on the train for nourishment; the drink is more of the wet your whistle size, and there are only two choices of shortbread cookie, vanilla or chocolate. In my opinion the Trenitalia vanilla cookie is better-tasting than the chocolate, which has an aftertaste not to my American liking.

Venice

In Venice, don't buy any items your first day if you're spending two days or more. Window shop only. The beautiful item in one store that you can't resist can be found, I guarantee it, in twenty other stores at a lower price. The lower prices can be found a few blocks from the main drag between Rialto and San Marco. I bought a charming drinking glass for $14 that was going for $30 on the seafront at San Marco and on the Rialto bridge. I'm drinking Diet Mountain Dew from it right now as I write this. How great is that?

Refrigerator magnets that were four euro on the main drag were one euro in other locations. The same ones.

Another thing about buying glass in Venice: they are well-practiced at packing glass and shipping even the most incredibly fragile things so they won't break. It could cost more than the item, but the heart wants what the heart wants. Be braced to expect shipping costs around $40 to $120, and two weeks later it will arrive.

In Venice, store prices are proportional to proximity to the tourist paths. Go down a skinny street for even 100 paces and prices are 30%-60% lower for exactly the same thing. Really, half the price for that cup, necklace, or face mask, just get away from the main areas and be prepared to peek into four or five shops before you spot it again. Few stores will accept a credit card transaction for under ten euro, mainly because credit cards work differently there, with a per-transaction charge rather than the 3% charge used in America. You'll have to carry around cash for all those less-than-ten euro expenditures. A nice restaurant with a six euro pizza and two euro house wine might only accept cash.

Venice is a city where mosquito repellent spray will be useful. If you forget it or don't want to crowd your liquids bag, buy it there.

Stupid questions about Venice (that I never found an answer to until I was there):

Do the vaporettos run after dark?

Yes. They have head lights just like cars. They don't run terribly late, maybe to midnight tops, and less frequently after 8 PM. If you're arriving by train before 10 PM, it is possible to take the vaporetto to a spot nearer to your hotel.

Can I walk?

Yes. Despite everything you read, Venice is a walk-everywhere town; a big pedestrian mall. It might look like the only way to get to a building is by water, but that is not true. That's the backside of every building. In fact, while buildings butt up against the canals, most can't be entered from that side.

Will it smell bad?

Yes and no. It depends on the month, the weather, and who knows what. All I can tell you is some visitors find the odor unbearable, yet in May 2013 I smelled nothing bad, only the occasional flowering vine. Some people say flooding and odor go hand in hand, but it was high water when I was there and there was no smell, even from the puddles.

Why are there so many boarded-up buildings?

The irony of Venice is that its world-wide reputation makes housing cost as much as New York—$350,000 for a one-bedroom, third floor walk-up condo. Yet even that isn't enough to fund what it would take to fix the structural defects in several-hundred-year-old buildings to make them safely habitable once again. When the builders were building, they weren't thinking four hundred years, they were thinking one hundred years. It's our own foolishness that insists we keep an old building merely because it's old. Sometimes they were built flimsily and then a few fancy windows and door frames were thrown on over that junk to please the buyer.

Result: building is uninhabitable by 2010, and fancy door frame rots away. Is this better? To me, it makes more sense to strip out all the good stuff and replace the building with one that is built to last 500 years. Then stick the 'good stuff' back onto the new building. I'm in the tiny minority with that opinion.

Scary-shabby-looking hotel in Venice, under the cheesy red circle. Ohmygawd-what-have-I-done?

Why does my hotel look so bad on the outside?

Most hotels in Venice are repurposed buildings. When they were built they were not hotels—they were residences, business offices, banks or stores. To become a hotel, interior walls were changed, and sometimes neighboring buildings were connected on one or more floors to have a bigger hotel. What the owners couldn't do was tear down the old building and start afresh like they would in Ohio. It's such a hassle to get city approval to make an exterior change that a learned helplessness develops. They don't

Same hotel, from inside looking out the door; charming canal views and free buffet breakfast.

improve, but they also don't wipe a rag.

Two of the hotels I stayed at in Italy had fist-sized signs at the door as the only signage. In Venice, the outside says nothing about the inside. When I walked up to the one shown here, it gave me visions of having purchased a metal cot with a flipped-over cardboard box for a nightstand, people groaning in pain in the background. The bars on the windows reminded me of too many prison movies. Don't judge a book by its cover.

Signage in Venice is all over and helpful

What if I get lost?

Turn that around: aim to get lost. What I mean is, the fun of Venice is wandering and exploring. It's a small island; eventually and too soon you'll either come to the canal or to the shore. Like a human pinball, go off in another direction. Explore, enjoy, pop in to whatever business establishment piques your interest. Find beautiful bridges; find ridiculously skinny roads; find dinky stores with lovely wares or delectable food and wine. Boats are nice, but this is a walking town.

When you're done having fun, find signage to either S. Marco, Rialto, or the train station. All you need to know is how to get to your hotel from one of those three.

Get that route firmly in your mind and you're never lost. Signage for the station may either say Santa Lucia, Ferrovia or strada ferrata. Most of the signage is handwritten on the walls who knows how long ago, so be sharp. See the S. Marco on the wall in front of my Hotel? That's not a joke, you really do squeeze into that space between the walls, and through a handful of other ones, and end up at St. Mark's Square.

WC sign over the door; these mean toilet, and cost about $2 per use. Use the one in the restaurant before you leave even if it isn't compelling.

Another tip: Most restaurants have a business card with a map on the back orienting their restaurant to one of those three locations. If you eat there, definitely ask for the card; it's a great souvenir. If you're lost, find a restaurant and ask for the card. If they don't have one, just move to the next. If you are on the way back to the train station and can't spot any signs, plan B is hit the restaurants for their

Alla Ferrovia means to the train station

business card/map, or just get directions from the host. They know.

The three and four hour tours to Murano and the other islands rush you around too much to sit down for a brew and enjoy the ambience, which I hear is nice. While it might make a nice day trip to take the vaporetto 41 (there) or 42 (back) for €13 round trip if you have five or six days in Venice, it's off the plate if you have under three days. With a vaporetto card, the trip is free. Many people write in travel reviews that the same Murano glass objects are sold for half the price in the plentiful glass shops in Venice, so don't go to Murano for the glass.

Murano glass is sold all over Venice, and the farther you are from the tourist paths between Rialto and San Marco, the more the price drops for the same stuff.

WC. Venice has pay potties, and they're not cheap. The signs for them say WC with an arrow. Just seeing the WC sign doesn't mean it's close; you could chase this signage for blocks. They're easy to walk right past and not know it until you notice the WC signs are pointing back to where you just were. Both the VeniceCard and the ACTV vaporetto card come with some potty visits, or they can be added.

Take advantage of free restroom facilities at restaurants after you dine.

Rome

There are about eight ways to get from Fiumicino – Leonardo da Vinci airport, and cost is roughly related to speed.

http://www.rome-airport.info/

Visit here for the latest on transportation choices. In Italy, it's good to have a plan B to switch to without too much trouble. In my case I wanted to take the Leonardo Express to Termini, the big train station which is also the hub of the subway system and where all the HOHO buses converge, but it was taking too long to find and I happened to be walking right by the Terravision Shuttles, so I took one of those to Termini instead. On the way back I took the Leonardo Express to the airport.

If saving money is a top priority, you can take the Metropolitan train, a lower cost solution, to the Tiburtina metro (subway) station and then navigate the subways to your first destination.

Buses are the slowest, and rush hour traffic in Rome is pretty bad. Cabs will suffer the same fate of being slower than the train. Even if you're a cab-everywhere person, from the airport into Rome is one time that taking the train may be quicker, smell nicer, and be a more comfortable ride.

There are actually lists for the top 100 things to see in Rome. That's too many to help you out. Aim for two to five things per day, depending upon proximity and your stamina.

That said, you can't go wrong marching through several of sites on a Top Ten list. Just google **Rome Top Ten** . . .and check out the sites, attractions and things to do. If your stay in Rome is longer than five days or this is your second or third trip you might add something not on a top ten list. Filter your choices based on knowing yourself. If you love beautiful art and sniff at half-knocked-down brick walls, then you know what to do. Personally, I came to view the half-knocked-down brick walls and dutifully took in a lot of overdone artwork. Painted ceilings grew on me, I have to admit. I still stare at the blank slates overhead in my house, wondering why I thought plain white was a good look all these years.

I brought opera glasses and spent over an hour in the Sistine Chapel examining every inch, a bucket list thing for me since I was about eight. Unbelievably, I have seen reviews of the same Vatican tour where the writer said it wasn't worth it because 1) the guide spoke with an accent and 2) there were a lot of people. Nothing else stuck in his mind. If you're that guy, please don't take up space in the Vatican, go have a beer or ride the HOHO.

If you wish a side effect of your Italy trip to be something to talk about with other people, do some of the top ten things in each place you visit.

Whether it's visiting coastlines, climbing tall buildings for the view, medieval art and antiquities, famous churches, homes of famous historical figures, taking bridge photos, Roman architecture and statuary, or you name it, having a theme and doing a little hunting for those sites makes you happier with the trip and more interesting when you return.

There are several overrated sites. One is the Spanish steps in Rome. If you're a movie buff, sure go there, but there are more worthy sites for archeological or meaningful history value. There are steps like this in front of half the courthouses in America.

Spanish Steps: Every face says "I'm here, what am I supposed to look at? Nothing? Really?!" Notice how the locals try to juice it up by adding a single palm tree and a few tubs of cheap flowers.

Trevi Fountain has huge crowds that linger longer than makes sense if the point is to examine the fountain or toss in their 'return to Rome' coins. The fountain appeared in a handful of 1950s and 60s movies. The ritual, dating from 1954, is to put your back toward the fountain and throw a coin with the right hand over the left shoulder into the water to ensure a return to Rome one day. Some opportunist changed the myth, so now one coin means return, two coins means a new romance, and three coins leads to marriage. The official story is that the city uses the money to fund a food bank for Rome's poor. This is where the pickpockets and bag slashers hang out.

Resist the urge to book each day solidly full of bases to touch, leaving only forty-five minutes for lunch, twenty-five minutes to take the subway from here to there, and so on right up to the two hour after-dark walking tour. Leave yourself elbow room. If you don't, one misstep and the whole day goes out of sync. A dead watch battery, a late train, a need to pop back to the hotel to change clothes, getting lost for twenty minutes or needing to find an ATM shouldn't blow the day's schedule out of the water. Schedule two or three things per day. Buy the tickets online ahead of time. Keep a list, with dots on maps, of optional things nearby. Blocking out two hours for lunch and three hours for dinner provides a bit of relaxation and flexibility.

Always, make the journey part of the itinerary. You aren't just walking eight blocks to a restaurant, you're exploring that neighborhood and its architecture. You aren't just taking the train from Rome to Florence, you're getting a panoramic view of Tuscany.

Guided package tours can do that kind of lockstep planning because they have worked out all the bugs. You have one shot at it. Space between events ensures each one will get done.

The Vatican Museums and Sistine Chapel

Going to Rome without seeing the Vatican is like going to Antarctica and not seeing a penguin. You'll have to explain why not to everyone from this day forward. Is that how you want the rest of your life to be?

Unless your group tour is taking care of it, buy tickets online for an official Vatican guided tour a few weeks ahead of your trip. Two months ahead is even better. What if you find the day you want to visit is shaded out, meaning all the tickets are sold?

What if you're a solo traveler—the Vatican books only parties of two or more.

Here's what you do: Hunt for other tour businesses that purchase blocks of tickets. Sites like ticketItaly.com, florencetours.net, darkrome.com, and Prestotours.com will sell to solo travelers and might have some left even when the Vatican website shows the day shaded out. I bought my ticket from florencetours.net. It cost a bit more than buying direct, but I went as a solo on a day listed as sold-out on the Vatican's website. What's $10 or $20 compared to not going at all?

Be aware that when you buy from the tour groups above, their canned email might contain totally different instructions than the fine print (which might be in Italian) on the voucher they ask you to print out. Read them both, but odds are the instructions on the voucher are the correct ones. Phone them for clarification if you are confused.

Vatican tours are given by only Vatican tour guides, regardless of who sold you the tour. No bare shoulders or bare legs; long pants or long skirt only. Only a small bag is allowed, no shopping bags, backpacks, or briefcase-size items. You are not allowed to take photos. You are allowed to 'talk' on the phone, if you catch my drift.

The Vatican museum is not near St. Peter's Basilica. Be sure you look at a map to arrive at the entrance to the museum. At night, the lit up Basilica is worth seeing.

The Vatican tickets require the paper copy, not a visual on a phone (that could change tomorrow). They give you instructions on what not to bring. Don't bring that stuff. I witnessed weeping women not allowed in because they didn't follow the instructions, and simply thought: good.

Shame on them. If anything, I think the guards allow the rules to bend too much. The artwork you'll see is too precious to let the backpack people in.

Bringing along a pair of opera glasses can be fun, to check it out at the brushstroke level.

The Colosseum

First off, there are several spellings for Colosseum and all of them are right. The ticket for the Colosseum is also good for the nearby ruins of the Forum and Palatine Hill the same day.

Buy the ticket or tour online so you can take your print-out to the much-shorter Groups line where you are issued the ticket.

Tip: if for some reason you didn't buy online, walk over to the Forum entrance to buy the shared ticket in that much-shorter line. Guided tours at several price points and times are available online as well as offered by guides at the entrance (although the latter may entail some sitting and waiting until enough customers are gathered).

The Colosseum Underground tours and Colosseum by Night tours are getting rave reviews. If one tour company doesn't offer it on the night you want to go, another might.

Near the Colosseum ticket office you can buy audio or video tours. They will want to keep your passport or driver's license hostage to ensure you return the unit—get used to it, a lot of museums do that. The video tour costs a dollar more than the mere audio tour and uses an iTouch to help you locate what they're talking about. It also shows movie clips featuring the Colosseum, which is charming, and it's amusingly obvious the filmmakers took a little artistic license. I chose the video tour, not a guided tour because my first major was archeology and I didn't want to be rushed, but if you're hearing it for the first time a guided tour is best. The exit is very far from the entrance and the only restrooms are on the exterior.

Florence

In Firenza, which is the real name, all the top attractions are within easy walking distance. Unlike most other cities where a hotel near the train station can be a practical choice depending upon your plans, in Firenza picking one a little more south and east, or closer to the river, can save you time.

Streets are so scary narrow that I don't recommend driving. Like in Rome, it isn't about avoiding hitting anything. Driving here is like a waltz; the other partners expect certain motions or speeds from you, a certain level of proceeding. If you hit the brakes there is a good chance a scooter or bicycle will hit you from the rear or side and say it's your fault.

Taxis cannot be hailed in Firenza; to get one you have to go to a Taxi stand or phone for a pickup. If you don't speak Italian, the hotel or B&B staff will be glad to call for you. Maps showing the Taxi stands can be found at the train station and most hotels. They can drop you off anywhere; without a phoned request, go to the nearest taxi stand to get one.

There are three doors on the ATAF buses, which are free with the Firenza Card: the front and back ones to enter and the middle one to exit. If you bought a ticket, as soon as you get on, head to the ticket validating machine to get a date stamp. The ticket is good for ninety minutes.

The street vendors in the main plazas, such as the Piazza della Repubblica, offer truly good bargains on leather goods, shoes, and scarves. Fine leather purses that might run $300 in the US can be had for $60. A large snakeskin purse that might cost $3,500 is sold here for €600 euro. A real snakeskin wallet runs €300 euro ($380) here; in the US, over $800.

In case you get any ideas of funding the trip via a few handbags, here are a few factors to consider:

It's not legal to become a free-lance importer. You would need to keep your purchases under the radar of customs and anyone rifling through your bags, which is a fact of life when commercial air flight is concerned. They are on the prowl for smugglers, which is the legal term for this activity.

The other factor is while stores might ask $3,500 for that purse, what are the odds that someone you show it to will love it enough to pay that much; purses are even more dependent upon personal taste than blouses or coffee cups. To sell a one-off out of your car trunk, people are going to want a discount from retail.

To play it out, say you buy five snakeskin purses for $750 US dollars and manage to get them out without raising any suspicions, but have to deeply discount two of them just to sell and can't move the last two at all. How many people can you scrape up who will spend $2,000 on a purse AND will buy when there's shady business going on? You'll have incurred all the stress of becoming an outlaw, of meeting strangers who are OK with shady dealings, all of this for a profit of what, perhaps $200?

Setting that aside, if you are considering buying a snakeskin purse, you could fly to Florence, buy it there, eat a nice steak dinner, fly back and be a few bucks ahead.

It's very worthwhile to use a bit of your annual clothes budget for belts and leather goods of all kinds while in Florence. Don't forget birthday, anniversary and holiday gifts too.

Some things, like scarfs and silk shopping bags, are worth getting not because of price, but because the selection is so huge. In a retail store, at any given time you might have twenty to pick from; here there are 800. You can get something that really represents your style and matches the colors you want to match.

The tunnel and the steps are streets on the map of Firenza; if you're new to town, driving can be tricky.

Italy is a wonderful place that I hope you and I will visit again. There are enough works of art, lavish old buildings, antiquities, delicious dishes and scrumptious desserts to fill a dozen vacations. This book is for that first or second trip, ensuring you have truly caught the high points. Later, there's time for isolated Tuscan Villas, browsing the less-traveled paths, and island hopping. Experiencing the best of Italy, if future circumstances conspire to make this the one and only trip, will be a lifelong treasure.

Have a great trip!

ABOUT THE AUTHOR

Thank you for reading my book. As a lifelong traveler, I can't get enough of reading and listening to the travels of others, what went right, and didn't.

What can suck all the fun out of a trip is often an extraordinarily tiny misstep, a momentary lapse of attention, or a simple misunderstanding of something familiar. The auto-pilot behaviors that serve us so well in ordinary life fail miserably while on vacation.

My son is used to traveling with me, used to our plans simply happening, so he has no idea of the measures I've taken to rein in runaway horses. For instance, we planned a five day trip to the Consumer Electronics Show, CES, in Las Vegas. Plane trouble had us stuck in Charlotte (free hotel, free food) for a day, plus another whole day taking flights through three other airports before finally arriving in Las Vegas moments before midnight. With multiple phone calls I rescheduled our trip to the Grand Canyon from Thursday to Saturday, and dinner at the Stratosphere from Wednesday to Friday, straightened out hotel issues, and we spent only one day at CES instead of two and a half. We had fun, did all the great stuff we planned to do, and it went fine. My son was unaware that it was a total disaster. Every single thing had to be managed, juggled and rescheduled on the fly. Without my printouts it couldn't have been done. In someone else's hands it could have been two days of sleeping on the airport floor, losing our Vegas hotel room, and never seeing the Grand Canyon.

Or Kitt Peak. This is my emblematic travel story. It started with my mistake. Kitt Peak is an observatory on top of a mountain in Arizona, the largest collection of optical telescopes in the world, and they give, as one would expect, evening tours. Somehow I wrote down the wrong address and zoomed in on the wrong part of Arizona, so my X on the map was fairly close to Tombstone, AZ. Because my high-school age son seemed interested in it, I planned to arrive early so we could tool around before the 6:30 PM evening tour began. When we arrived at the location after 5:00, it plumb wasn't there. My son used his phone to get the right address, and the GPS put us one hundred miles away—and worse than that, the shortest way there was going through Tucson at rush hour.

My son went a bit ballistic that a thing he'd looked forward to just went pifft. I kicked into high gear. While heading there, I had him fish out the phone number from my printouts and dial for me. We reached the receptionist seconds before she left for the day; another two minutes and no one would have answered the phone. She called over the fellow who would give the tour, and he told me they eat, drink and watch a video, not actually going up to the telescopes until 7:30. More than that, the lower gate closed automatically at 6:30, but he adjusted the programming to keep it open for us. He said he'd wait for us, and also gave me his personal cell phone and asked that I call when I passed the gate so he could lock it.

I did what it took to get there. What I hadn't expected was the narrow road winding up the mountain, with drops of thousands of feet just six inches off the pavement. I knew two things: 1) I can drive without crossing over the white stripe, especially if there is no oncoming traffic; 2) If I look sideways even once, I will pee in my pants and slow to five MPH. I went up the mountain at 40 MPH, forcing my eyes to the cliff side the whole way. My son was so panicked—he was looking over the edge three feet from the wheels— that I ordered him to close his eyes. We arrived in time to munch a sandwich and drink a juice and catch the end of the video. The tour was our first time viewing the planets and galaxies through several telescopes; enchanting.

This could be just a funny story about mom speeding and not getting a ticket. Not exactly; years later, my son chose Physics for a major and wants to be an Astrophysicist.

Carrying along printouts with all the phone numbers, directions, and addresses that are already stashed in the phone, setting PINs for credit cards even when you intend to use your ATM card, taking extra time to make a list and touch each item can seem a huge waste of time. Until it isn't. For me— maybe I'm just extremely accident-prone—one or more of these measures turn out to be trip-savers 50% of the time.

The thing about preventing bad stuff is that it's hard to get credit for it. Like mounting a handrail on staircase, if ten years later no one ever broke a leg on those steps, was it a waste of money? Preventing is the most thankless task in the whole world.

If this book was useful to you, please check out my other books: Contractor Heaven, Negotiating When Money Matters: Home Improvement, Fixing It Fast and Fine: Home Repair for Real Estate Agents, Getting the Best Price on a Used Car, and the latest on air travel, Flying For First Timers.

www.gettingbestprice.com